Murder On The Nile

A play

Agatha Christie

Samuel French — London
New York - Toronto - Hollywood

CHARACTERS

(in the order of their appearance)

1st BEADSELLER.
2nd BEADSELLER.
STEWARD.
MISS FFOLIOT-FFOULKES.
CHRISTINA GRANT.
SMITH.
LOUISE.
DR. BESSNER.
KAY MOSTYN.
SIMON MOSTYN.
CANON PENNEFATHER.
JACQUELINE DE SEVERAC.
McNAUGHT.

SYNOPSIS OF SCENES.

The scene is laid throughout in the observation saloon of the paddle steamer *Lotus* on the Nile between Shellal and Wadi Halfa.

ACT I.   At Shellal.   Late afternoon.

ACT II.   SCENE 1.   By the Temple of Abu Simbel.   Three days later.   Evening, after dinner.

SCENE 2.   The same.   Five minutes later.

ACT III.   The same.   The next morning.

MURDER ON THE NILE

ACT I.

SCENE.—*The forward observation saloon of the steamer "Lotus" at Shellal. Late afternoon.*

The saloon is glass enclosed so as to give a full view of the river panorama. Doorways down stage R *and* L *give access to the decks. Below them are more windows through which those about to enter can be seen before they have opened the doors. The decks are supposed to run aft and forward, but not round the bow. All the cabins, etc., are supposed to be aft of the stage. The gangway to the shore is off* R *so that all new arrivals come on from* R.

The saloon is arranged like a lounge with wicker chairs grouped round tables. At C *there is a biggish table with magazines on it. Various travel folders and posters are attractively displayed. A passenger list is pinned up on a pillar between the windows up* C.

(See the Ground Plan for the detailed arrangement of the furniture.)

When the CURTAIN *rises two picturesque* BEADSELLERS, *laden with fly-whisks, beads, postcards, and scarabs, are chatting in Arabic with a Nubian* STEWARD, *who wears long white robes and a tarboosh and has a coal-black face. He is always smiling and amiable, and understands about a quarter of what the passengers say to him. All three are in fits of laughter. Suddenly the* STEWARD *straightens up and shoos away the* BEADSELLERS *as the noise of approaching porters is heard from off* R. 1ST BEADSELLER *goes off* R. 2ND BEADSELLER *moves to the door* L. *The* STEWARD *moves below the table* C.

MISS FFOLIOT-FFOULKES *and* CHRISTINA GRANT *enter* R *with* 1ST BEADSELLER *in close attendance.* MISS FFOLIOT-FFOULKES *is wearing a topee and tourist clothes. She is sixty, snobbish, and bad-tempered. She comes below the chair* R *of the* C *table.* CHRISTINA *is a nice sensible girl with an amazingly equable temper. She is carrying* MISS FFOLIOT-FFOULKES' *coat and dressing case. She comes to the table down* L *and puts the coat on it.* 2ND BEADSELLER *exits* L.

STEWARD. Good afternoon, ladies. Good afternoon. Welcome to *Lotus.*

BEADSELLER *(moving to* MISS FFOLIOT-FFOULKES' R *elbow).* See, lady—see ! Lapis—real lapis—real amber—very nice, very cheap. Look, lady, real scarab, big King Rameses !

*(*MISS FFOLIOT-FFOULKES *waves him away. He transfers to* CHRISTINA.*)*

MISS FFOLIOT-FFOULKES. Miss ffoliot-ffoulkes and Miss Grant.

STEWARD. Oh, yes, I have very nice cabins for you. Fifteen and sixteen. Nicest cabins on boat.

MISS FFOLIOT-FFOULKES. Take us there, please. (*The* STEWARD *starts to cross towards* CHRISTINA *for the coat.*) Christina, you've not dropped my coat? (CHRISTINA *crosses the* BEADSELLER *to* R *of the* STEWARD *who attempts to take the coat from her.*) Don't let him have it. Carry it yourself.

CHRISTINA. I have it. (*She crosses* L *towards the door.*)

BEADSELLER (*coming down stage between the* STEWARD *and* MISS FFOLIOT-FFOULKES). Look, lady—real lapis—scarab. King Rameses!

MISS FFOLIOT-FFOULKES. No, no, I don't want anything.

BEADSELLER (*crossing to* CHRISTINA). You like go donkey riding when you come back? I give you card. I got very good donkey. My donkey "Whisky and Soda"—that very good donkey. (*To* MISS FFOLIOT-FFOULKES.) You like postcard? I got all kinds of postcards.

(MISS FFOLIOT-FFOULKES *turns away up* R *of the* C *table; the* BEAD-SELLER *follows her.*)

You English lady? King George, Queen Elizabeth—hip, hip, hooray! Very nice postcard—Temple of Philae, Tomb King Tutankhamen, English Church Cairo . . .

(*The* STEWARD *makes an onslaught on the* BEADSELLER *in furious Arabic. The* BEADSELLER *goes off* R.)

STEWARD (*crossing below the* C *table of the door* L). You come this way.

(*He exits* L. MISS FFOLIOT-FFOULKES *and* CHRISTINA *follow him.* SMITH *enters* R. *He is followed by the* BEADSELLER. SMITH *is a rather dirty-looking young man in grey flannel trousers and an open shirt. His voice belies his appearance. As he enters he waves the* BEADSELLER *aside and crosses up* C.)

BEADSELLER (*persisting*). Very hot postcards? You like see girls dancing—real native dance? . . . (*Persisting.*) I take you duck shooting? Good sport? You English gentleman? American? Parley Francais? German? Italian? Russian? Swiss? Yugoslavian? No? (SMITH *shakes his head and continues to the door.*) What you nationality?

SMITH. Japanese!

(*He goes out* L. *The* BEADSELLER *remains with mouth open.*)

BEADSELLER. Japanese? (*He shakes his head in utmost perplexity.*)

(LOUISE, *a good-looking French maid, enters* R. *The* BEADSELLER *crosses to her.*)

BEADSELLER. You like nice beads? Very cheap? Très gentille. Très chic.

LOUISE. No, no, I do not want anything.

(*The* BEADSELLER *exits* R. MISS FFOLIOT-FFOULKES *and* CHRISTINA *behind her, still carrying the dressing case and coat, enter* L. LOUISE *discreetly edges out* R.)

MISS FFOLIOT-FFOULKES (*crossing to the chair* R *of the* C *table and sitting*). It's absurd to say those are the best cabins on the boat. I don't believe it. You haven't left my little dressing case behind?

(SMITH *enters* L *and sits at the table down* L *with a magazine.*)

CHRISTINA. No, Aunt Helen, I have it here. (*She moves to the chair above the table* C.)

(MISS FFOLIOT-FFOULKES *looks round the saloon, her glasses sweep over* SMITH *as though he were a vaguely distasteful beetle.*)

MISS FFOLIOT-FFOULKES. I suppose this is where the passengers sit most of the time. (*With a look at* SMITH.) Reserved, I presume, for the use of *first* class passengers.

SMITH. All one class on this boat.

CHRISTINA. There's another lounge at the back of the boat.

SMITH. Stern.

MISS FFOLIOT-FFOULKES (*rising and moving to the window up* C). But this is where one will get the best view. (*She finds a pinned up paper on a pillar.*) Ah, a list of passengers. One likes to know who are going to be one's fellow travellers. On a boat like this one can't get away from people. So it means one has to be very careful.

SMITH (*cheerfully*). Or else one may get contaminated. (MISS FFOLIOT-FFOULKES *turns a cold eye on him.*) Don't mind me. I'm afraid I've got a habit of butting in.

(MISS FFOLIOT-FFOULKES *detaches the list. She comes back to the chair* R *of the* C *table and sits.* CHRISTINA *sits in the chair above the table.* SMITH *sprawls in his chair with his magazine.*)

MISS FFOLIOT-FFOULKES (*reading*). Now let me see. Canon Ambrose Pennefather. That sounds quite nice. I wonder if he's one of the Yorkshire Pennefathers? Of course one never knows in the Church nowadays. Hm! Dr. Bessner—foreign! Mr. William Smith—

SMITH. Negligible!

(CHRISTINA *nearly laughs.*)

MISS FFOLIOT-FFOULKES. Miss ffoliot-ffoulkes—dear me, they've spelt it with a big "F."

SMITH (*shaking his head gently*). Lèse-majesté.

MISS FFOLIOT-FFOULKES. Miss Christina Grant. Mr. and Mrs. Simon Mostyn and maid—why—I do believe that must be Kay Ridgeway!

CHRISTINA. Oh, Aunt Helen, how exciting! Do you think it's really her?

MISS FFOLIOT-FFOULKES. On her honeymoon, I suppose.

CHRISTINA. That must be it. The wedding was a fortnight ago. I read all about it in *The Tatler* at the hotel.

MISS FFOLIOT-FFOULKES. Well really, that will be *most* interesting. They say she threw over Lord Edgbaston to marry this young Mostyn. He is one of the Devonshire Mostyns—poor as a rat. (*The* STEWARD *enters* R.) Steward, come here. I don't like my cabin.

STEWARD (*coming down* RC; *smiling*). Very nice cabin. Very good. Get all afternoon sun.

MISS FFOLIOT-FFOULKES. That's exactly what I complain of. It will be too hot.

STEWARD. No, no, very nice breeze when boat go. Very pleasant.

MISS FFOLIOT-FFOULKES. I want cabins on this side of boat. (*She points* R.)

STEWARD. All right. I show you. (*He moves to the door* R.)

(MISS FFOLIOT-FFOULKES *gets up and goes to the door* R. CHRISTINA *rises*.)

MISS FFOLIOT-FFOULKES. Stay here, Christina. I don't want my things left. (*To the* STEWARD.) Is all the drinking water on this boat very fresh—is it boiled ?

(*She exits* R, *followed by the* STEWARD.)

SMITH (*after a pause*). Too bad they spelt your aunt's name with a large "F."

CHRISTINA. Oh, that's always happening. It's not really sensible when you come to think of it, to spell a name with two small "f's."

SMITH. It's one of our incomprehensible English whimsies. (*Pause.*) Are you going to Wadi Halfa and back for the trip, or on to Khartoum ?

CHRISTINA. Oh, just for the trip. It's all so picturesque, and I love the donkeys and all the beads and things. (*She takes a large plaster scarab out of her bag.*) I bought this yesterday. (*She crosses to* SMITH.) The man said it was a real sacred scarab. Is it ?

SMITH (*examining it*). The curious thing is that you couldn't buy one of these in Birmingham if you tried.

CHRISTINA. Oh, is that where it comes from ?

SMITH. I've always understood they were made in Birmingham for the export market, but it *may* be Sheffield.

CHRISTINA (*looking downhearted*). I paid five piastres for it.

SMITH. Anyway, it's a lovely specimen. So *naïve*, if you know what I mean.

(*There are noises from off* R. *The* BEADSELLERS *can be heard among them.*)

CHRISTINA (*moving up* C *and looking off* R). Somebody else is coming on board. I wonder if it's her ?

SMITH. You are expecting a friend ?

CHRISTINA. Oh, no. I meant Mrs. Mostyn. (*She crosses* RC.) She's on her honeymoon. You must have read about her : Kay Ridgeway. Her father was the great financier. They say she's the richest girl in England.

SMITH. That must be very bad for her.

CHRISTINA. She's not only rich. She's absolutely lovely ! And she's just made a romantic marriage. Think of being rich, and lovely, and having everything in the world you want ! (*Her tone is ecstatic.*)

SMITH. I'd rather not think of it. It makes me feel sick.

CHRISTINA. There have been pictures of her in all the papers.

SMITH (*rising and moving up* L ; *with fury*). Why should there be ? Why should anyone want to look at pictures of an idle, useless girl who's never done a hand's turn in her life ? Faugh ! Why not pictures of decent factory girls going to their day's work ?

CHRISTINA (*moving in to the* C *table; amused*). Who'd want to look at pictures of them ? I wouldn't.

SMITH (*turning on her*). Do you despise the workers of the world ?

CHRISTINA. Not at all. (*She sits on the corner of the table.*) I'm one myself. I work in an office in Edinburgh as a shorthand typist. But I wouldn't pay good money for a paper to look at pictures of shorthand typists or factory girls.

SMITH. You've no proper sense of the dignity of labour.

CHRISTINA. Do you do such an awful lot of work yourself ?

SMITH (*turning away down* L ; *slightly disconcerted*). I'm studying conditions at the moment. I intend to work extremely hard.

CHRISTINA. Well, maybe when you do, you'll understand that there's such a thing as romance. And when a rich girl like Kay Ridgeway, who might have married anybody, marries a young man with no money at all and very good-looking, and they're on their honeymoon and going to be on the same boat—well, it's just too thrilling for words.

SMITH. I see. You've got what used to be called the novelette mind.

CHRISTINA (*placidly*). There's no call to be *rude*. (*She moves to the window up* LC.)

(Dr. BESSNER *enters* R. *He is stout and middle-aged with spectacles. He has a marked foreign accent. He is earnestly repelling the two* BEADSELLERS.)

DR. BESSNER (*as he enters*). No, I do not want them. Those beads you have there, they are a very bad imitation—very bad, indeed.

(*The* STEWARD *suddenly appears from off* R *and drives off the* BEADSELLERS.)

DR. BESSNER (*moving to* RC). Very troublesome they are, these people. It is like the flies. All the time they are saying "Baksheesh ! Baksheesh !" (*Bringing his heels together, to* SMITH.) Dr. Bessner.

SMITH. William Smith.

(DR. BESSNER *bows and looks at* CHRISTINA.)

Miss—

CHRISTINA (*turning and coming to the chair* L *of the* C *table*). Grant.

(DR. BESSNER *gives a very correct bow and looks at her with approval.*)

DR. BESSNER. It is the first time you make upon the Nile this so agreeable voyage ?

CHRISTINA. Yes, it is the first time I've ever been in Egypt.

DR. BESSNER. There is in Egypt much of interest to be seen. The civilisation of Egypt was fine, very fine, and owing to action of sand and dry climate, much has been preserved to us. We will make stops and go on the shore and interesting temples visit. (*He beams on* CHRISTINA.) My Baedeker if you like I lend you. (*He crosses below the table to* CHRISTINA.)

SMITH. There's a thrilling offer for you.

CHRISTINA (*to* DR. BESSNER). Thank you very much. That's very kind of you.

DR. BESSNER.   A pleasure it will be.

(LOUISE *enters* L.   *She looks round, then goes out again* R *flinging a provocative glance at* SMITH *as she does so.*)

SMITH.   Ah ! Luscious female with the glad eye.   I'm glad someone appreciates me.

(MISS FFOLIOT-FFOULKES *enters* R.)

MISS FFOLIOT-FFOULKES (*to* CHRISTINA).   I've got a much better cabin now.   I *know* that man was trying to do for me.   The one for you next door is rather small—but it will do quite well.

(CHRISTINA *crosses above the* C *table towards* MISS FFOLIOT-FFOULKES.)

DR. BESSNER (*to* CHRISTINA).   Present me, please.

CHRISTINA (*rather nervously*).   Er—er, Mr. B-b-besser, my aunt.

DR. BESSNER.   Doctor Bessner.

(MISS FFOLIOT-FFOULKES *gives him a cold look, a tiny bow, and turns her back on him.*)

MISS FFOLIOT-FFOULKES (*moving to the table up* R).   I'm not at all satisfied with what that man says about the water.   (*She sits* R *of the table.*)   I don't believe they *do* boil it.   He had a very shifty look in his eye.   I've ordered some Evian—but I sometimes suspect that they just fill those up from a *tap.*   You'll have to boil some on the spirit lamp, Christina.

CHRISTINA.   Yes, Aunt Helen.

MISS FFOLIOT-FFOULKES.   You can unpack for me presently.

CHRISTINA.   I'll go and start now.

MISS FFOLIOT-FFOULKES.   Certainly not.   It's safer to keep the cases locked until the boat starts.   There are some suspicious looking characters hanging about.

CHRISTINA.   Just as you like.   (*She sits* L *of the table up* R.)

MISS FFOLIOT-FFOULKES.   And don't take out too much—until we see whether the stewards are honest.

(*The* STEWARD *enters* L *and crosses to* R.   MISS FFOLIOT-FFOULKES *stares at him.   He exits* R.)

DR. BESSNER (*moving up* L *and above the table* C ; *kindly and instructive*).   You have here the peoples of Nubia.   They are not, you see, of the same race.   Nubian peoples . . .

MISS FFOLIOT-FFOULKES (*ignoring* DR. BESSNER ; *raising her voice without looking at him*).   You might give me my *Life of Madame Recamier*, Christina.   Now where are my spectacles—Ah, I have them in my bag.

(KAY MOSTYN *enters* R *followed by* SIMON.   *There is a good deal of accompanying noise, and the two* BEADSELLERS *are pestering them. They carry on their conversation with punctuations of, "*You like nice lapis,*" etc., and cards and postcards thrust on them.* SIMON *is a good-looking, good-tempered young man of twenty-eight, with rather a simple,* *hearty manner.* KAY *is a beautiful young woman of twenty-four, dressed in expensive though simple clothes, and with the assured manner of one born to command. She comes down* RC.)

SIMON (*following* KAY). Well, here we are.

KAY (*moving below the table* C). What a frightful din ! Get rid of these creatures, Simon.

SIMON (*turning on the* BEADSELLERS). Whoosh ! Get out.

(*He shoos them through the door* R.)

KAY. Give them some money and tell them to go away.

(*The* STEWARD *enters* R.)

STEWARD. Mr. and Mrs. Mostyn ! Welcome to the *Lotus.* You'd like to see your cabins ? (*He comes to the chair* R *of the table* C.)

KAY. Has my maid got here ?

STEWARD. Maid ? Yes, she arrived half an hour ago with your luggage.

(LOUISE *enters* R *quickly.*)

KAY. Ah, there you are, Louise.

LOUISE (*coming down* RC). Yes, Madame. Everything is ready for you, Madame.

SIMON (*coming down* R *of* LOUISE). No difficulty in getting away ?

LOUISE (*with a faint insolence in the smile she gives him*). Oh, no, Monsieur. Everything was quite satisfactory. (*She gives him a sly glance.*) Monsieur need not be uneasy.

SIMON (*shortly*). Good.

LOUISE (*still insinuating a sly understanding*). I did everything, Monsieur, just as Monsieur told me.

SIMON (*brusquely*). Then that's all right. (*To* KAY.) Shall we go and look at the cabins ?

KAY. Yes, we'd better see they're all right. Take this, Louise. (*She gives her wrap to* LOUISE *and crosses her to* SIMON.)

(*The* STEWARD *goes out* R. KAY *and* SIMON *follow.* LOUISE *stands aside and then follows, making grimaces.*)

SMITH (*to the air*). Quite like royalty.

CHRISTINA. Oh, isn't she lovely ?

SMITH. Pity they forgot the red carpet.

(*The two* BEADSELLERS *crowd in again* R.)

1ST BEADSELLER (*crossing down stage to* SMITH). You like nice beads ? You like postcard ? All gentlemen like postcard. I show you.

SMITH. Go away.

1ST BEADSELLER (*crossing below the table and·up to* CHRISTINA). I take you donkey riding. My donkey "Whisky and Soda." Very good donkey.

2ND BEADSELLER (*elbowing the* 1ST BEADSELLER *aside*). No, no, you take my donkey, lady. His donkey very bad donkey—that donkey fall down. My donkey "Whoopadaisy," my donkey good donkey. You take my card—you have good donkey not fall down. Hip hip hooray— very good, very nice. God save the King.

(*The* STEWARD *enters* R *and shoos the* BEADSELLERS *off* R.)

DR. BESSNER (*crossing towards the* STEWARD). I would my cabin like to see. Number nineteen, Dr. Bessner.

STEWARD. Welcome to *Lotus*. You come this way. (*He leads the way across down stage to the door* L.) Very nice cabin—get all afternoon sun. Come this way, please.

(DR. BESSNER *follows the* STEWARD *and they go out* L.)

MISS FFOLIOT-FFOULKES. My dear Christina—do try to have a little more *savoir-faire*. I know you have not had many advantages in your upbringing, but the first thing to learn when you are travelling is *not* to rush into conversation with every single person you meet. Foreigners, in especial, are very trying. They are slower than an English person to see when they are not wanted.

(*The* BEADSELLERS *are heard from off* R.)

CHRISTINA. Those awful beadsellers are coming back again.

MISS FFOLIOT-FFOULKES. They ought not to be allowed on the boat.

SMITH (*moving up* C). They've got another victim. Now what kind of a fellow passenger have we got? (*He looks towards the door* R *and exclaims loudly in disgust.*) God, a parson!

(*He turns and goes out in disgust* L *as* CANON PENNEFATHER *enters* R. *He is a large imposing cleric of middle age.*)

MISS FFOLIOT-FFOULKES. A very ill-bred young man!

(CANON PENNEFATHER *turns at the door* R *and addresses a few sharp words in Arabic to the* BEADSELLERS. *They depart.* CANON PENNEFATHER *looks round smiling. He crosses up* C *and studies the view through the centre window.* MISS FFOLIOT-FFOULKES *eyes him with approval. When he at last turns, she is ready.*)

MISS FFOLIOT-FFOULKES. Very warm, is it not?

CANON (*courteously*). Yes, indeed. A particularly airless afternoon.

MISS FFOLIOT-FFOULKES. As we are fellow-travellers, I must introduce myself. I am Miss ffoliot-ffoulkes and this is my niece, Christina Grant. (*She is all butter and sweetness.*)

CANON (*pleasantly*). Ah, yes, indeed, these small boats are friendly affairs. I am Canon Pennefather.

MISS FFOLIOT-FFOULKES. One of the Yorkshire Pennefathers?

CANON (*smiling*). The Shropshire branch. (*A pause.*) We shall have a most beautiful view as we go up the Nile. These observation saloons are excellent ideas.

CHRISTINA. I'd like it better if it hadn't got a roof.

CANON. You'd find the sun much too hot, my dear young lady, beating down on your head.

(1ST BEADSELLER *enters* R.)

BEADSELLER (*crossing to the* CANON). You like bead, lapis, amber scarabs.

CANON. Nothing at all.

BEADSELLER. I show you postcards.

CANON. No.

BEADSELLER. I show you *holy* postcards. Old Coptic Church. Very early Christians—very nice, very holy.

CANON. Wonderful how persistent they are. And how they suit their wares to their company.

BEADSELLER. I got other postcards. (*He leers.*) Very nice . . .

(*The* STEWARD *enters* L. *He shoos off the* BEADSELLER *as he crosses to* CANON PENNEFATHER.)

STEWARD. Canon Pennefather? Welcome to *Lotus*. I show you cabin. Best cabin on boat.

MISS FFOLIOT-FFOULKES. It gets all the afternoon sun! (*She rises.*) Christina, I think I will go to *my* cabin. Bring my coat and the little handbag.

(*She goes out* R. CHRISTINA *rises. The* STEWARD *crosses to the door* L *and exits.* CANON PENNEFATHER *follows him to the door.*)

CANON (*turning at the door; courteously to* CHRISTINA). Au revoir, Miss Grant. We shall meet again later.

(CHRISTINA *crosses to him and speaks in a low voice.*)

CHRISTINA. I hope you won't think that young man was meaning to be rude who was here when you came in. I'm afraid you must have heard him. It's just a way he has. He doesn't really mean anything by it.

CANON (*smiling*). Some people dislike a clergyman travelling on a ship —they say it brings bad luck. But I don't think that will apply on our paddle steamer.

MISS FFOLIOT-FFOULKES (*off; calling*). Christina—Christina!

(CANON PENNEFATHER *goes out* L. CHRISTINA *hurries out* R. *After a pause,* KAY *enters slowly from off* R *and stands in the doorway a minute, presumably looking at the shore. She sighs as though relieved and moves into the saloon. She crosses to the window up* C. *She drops her bag into the chair* L *of the table up* R *as she passes. She stands for a moment looking out of the window, then glances at her wrist watch.* SIMON *enters* R. *He has a drink in his hand. He moves to the table up* R, *puts down his glass, and crosses to* R *of* KAY *and stands beside her with his hand on her shoulder. They are silent for a minute or two.*)

SIMON (*softly and caressingly*). Satisfied, my sweet?

KAY. Yes—yes! (*She gives a sigh.*) I'm going to enjoy this.

SIMON. So am I. (*He pauses.*) My lovely wife! (*He gives a quick glance round, then kisses her.*)

KAY. Did you ask if there were any more passengers to come on board?

SIMON. Yes. Everyone's arrived.

KAY. Then the boat could start. Go and arrange with the captain, or whoever it is, to start at once.

SIMON. It's not due to leave for half-an-hour.

KAY. Nonsense. Tell them to start now.

SIMON. I suppose it has to run to schedule.

KAY. Not at all. It will be just a question of a tip—that's all. It always is. (*She laughs at his doubtful face.*) You don't know the world as well as I do, Simon. It's usually just a question of how much.

(CANON PENNEFATHER *comes in* L *and stands in the doorway, watching them. They do not see him.*)

SIMON (*turning away and crossing down* R). I don't quite like doing that.

KAY (*following him down* R). Darling, don't be pig-headed. (*As she passes the chair she picks up her bag.*) I want to get off as soon as possible.

(CANON PENNEFATHER *exits* L.)

SIMON. It's quite all right, Kay. Louise says so.

KAY. Louise isn't always as clever as she thinks she is.

SIMON. I rather wish you'd get rid of that girl, Kay. She's got a nasty way of looking at you sometimes.

KAY (*carelessly*). Probably hates me—though I don't see why she should. I give her heaps of things. But I couldn't possibly part with her. (*She takes the mirror from her bag and uses it.*) She's simply marvellous with hair and nails and all that.

SIMON. I'd be your lady's maid, Kay!

KAY. I wonder what I'd look like with your great clumsy fingers in my hair!

SIMON. Nothing could prevent you looking the loveliest thing on God's earth. Enjoying your honeymoon?

CANON (*off* L). Thank you! Thank you!

(*He enters* L.)

KAY (*putting the mirror back in her bag*). I'm going. (*She turns* L *and sees* CANON PENNEFATHER. *She looks quite stupefied.*) Why! Uncle Ambrose!

(CANON PENNEFATHER *crosses to her below the table* C. *They meet down* RC.)

CANON (*sounding equally dumbfounded*). Kay! My dear child! What an extraordinary surprise!

(SMITH *enters quietly* L. *He sits in the chair* L *of the table up* L *with a magazine.*)

KAY. I thought you were in Palestine.

CANON. So I was, last week.

(SMITH *looks at* CANON PENNEFATHER *sideways.*)

KAY. I wrote to you—to the King David Hotel at Jerusalem. Didn't you get my letter?

CANON. I changed my plans.

KAY (*a little embarrassed*). Then you don't know—

CANON. Know what?

KAY. That I'm married.

(CANON PENNEFATHER *looks at her in stupefaction*.)

CANON. Married?

KAY (*laughing and confused*). Yes—to Simon. (*She turns to* SIMON.) (SIMON *comes forward*.) Simon Mostyn. Simon, this is my guardian—Father's dearest friend—My Uncle Ambrose by courtesy.

(CANON PENNEFATHER *crosses* KAY *to* SIMON. KAY *breaks below the table*.)

SIMON (*shaking hands*). I've heard a lot about you, sir. (*He grins in a friendly fashion*.)

CANON. We have never actually met—but I've seen you before.

SIMON (*vaguely*). Have you? So you never heard about our marriage?

CANON (*turning to* KAY ; *sitting* R *of the table* C). It must have been very sudden, Kay?

KAY (*sitting on the* C *table; guiltily*). Well—we didn't waste any time. I hope, darling, that you're not terribly hurt that we didn't wait for you to come back and marry us. But I didn't really know how long your Holy Land tour was going to last . . . and anyway I'm over twenty-one, so I hadn't to ask your legal consent—and I *did* write you a *very* nice letter telling you all about Simon and everything—which it seems was just wasted labour, because you never got it !

CANON. I shall get it some day, I expect.

KAY. I thought it would be sure to catch you at the hotel in Jerusalem. But what a coincidence that you should actually be here—on this boat.

CANON. Indeed, Kay, you know I always believe that there is no such thing as chance.

KAY. Anyhow, it's lovely that you're here. (*Firmly*.) And now you and Simon can have a drink together and make friends. I'm going to change. See you later, darling.

(*She goes out* R.)

SIMON. What will you have, sir? (*He turns to the window down* R *and presses a bell beside it*.) I gather from what Kay said that you're not a teetotaler.

CANON. No, I am of the worldly order of clergy, who enjoy the good things of this life. Take a little wine for thy stomach's sake has always struck me as sound advice. (*He laughs conventionally*.)

SMITH (*snorting angrily*). Stomach's sake, that's good !

(*He rises and goes out* L. *There is a pause.* SIMON *takes a cigarette and lights it*.)

SIMON. I—I hope you don't mind my marrying Kay, sir. I mean, I hope that you'll think I'm good enough for her—not that I could ever really be that. She's such an amazing creature.

CANON. As I said, I've seen you before, Mr. Móstyn.

SIMON. Make it Simon, won't you, sir? I'm afraid, you know, that I don't quite remember where—

CANON. I don't think you would remember—under the circumstances.

(*The* STEWARD *enters* L.)

STEWARD. Did you ring, sir ?

SIMON (*to* CANON PENNEFATHER). What will you have, sir ?

CANON. I think perhaps a gin-fizz.

SIMON (*to the* STEWARD). Make it two. (*He moves up* R *and picks up his glass.*)

(*The* STEWARD *exits* L.)

SIMON (*coming down* RC). You were saying— ?

CANON. I was saying that I once saw you at a small restaurant in London. The Château en Espagne. You were sitting at the next table to me. I could not help hearing your conversation.

SIMON. Yes ?

CANON (*with emphasis*). There was a very striking looking girl with you—a dark girl. You were talking of a time to come—when you would go for your honeymoon—to Egypt.

SIMON (*moving up* R *and crossing to up* LC ; *drawing a deep breath*). Oh, I see. (CANON PENNEFATHER *watches him very closely.*) You feel—that that needs some explanation ?

CANON. Frankly, yes. It was not so very long ago.

SIMON (*turning angrily*). I suppose you think I married Kay for her money. Well, you're wrong. I'd have gone after Kay to the world's end if she hadn't had a penny piece. (*He pauses. His manner changes.*) As a matter of fact, I'm rather glad you *did* see us in the Château en Espagne. It makes it easier for me to tell you the whole thing—and God knows I want to tell it to someone. (*He moves to the chair above the* C *table.*)

CANON (*encouragingly*). Yes ?

SIMON. The girl you saw me with was Jacqueline de Severac. I was engaged to her. She was also Kay's best friend.

CANON. I see.

SIMON (*sitting in the chair above the* C *table*). Don't misunderstand me. I'd never met Kay then, but I'd heard Jackie talk about her. They'd been at school together at some snob place in Paris. Then Jackie's people lost all their money and she and Kay didn't see each other very often. But they wrote, and Kay was just as fond of Jackie as ever. She would have given her all sorts of things only Jackie was too proud to take them.

(*The* STEWARD *enters with two drinks. He places them on the table at* SIMON'S R. SIMON *signs a chit.* CANON PENNEFATHER *takes a drink.* SIMON *takes his, rises, and moves to* LC. *The* STEWARD *exits* L.)

Well, there we were, both poor as church mice—and I was out of a job as well. Things were looking rather blue—and then Jackie heard that Kay's agent, who looked after her Yorkshire property, had died, and it seemed it would be a marvellous chance for me. I'm good at that sort of thing— I'm country bred. So she rushed off to Kay—and Kay, like the sport she is, said of course she'd give Jackie's fiancé the job. (*He pauses.*) So I took it—cheerio. (*He raises his glass.*)

CANON (*drinks*). And then ?

(SIMON *puts his glass on the table down* L *and turns to* CANON PENNEFATHER.)

SIMON (*earnestly*). That's what I've got to make you understand, sir. The moment I saw Kay—it was all over. Jackie didn't exist any more. I'm every sort of swine you like to call me—but that's how it was. I had loved Jackie in a kind of way—but when Kay came—oh, it was like the moon when the sun comes out—you just don't see the moon any more.

CANON. Not a bad simile.

SIMON. That's how it was. Kay was the sun . . . I tried to fight against it—but it was no good. And when I found she felt the same . . . (*He stops and shakes his head, bereft of words.*)

CANON. And Miss de Severac ?

SIMON. Jackie took it hard—very hard, indeed. Of course I know I treated her—very badly.

CANON. You and Kay.

SIMON (*sitting* R *of the* C *table; quickly*). Kay had nothing to do with it. It wasn't her fault. I was just feeling—well—restless, and then I met Kay and she just swept me off my feet. I'd never seen anyone so lovely . . . It was all so amazing. Everyone kow-towing to her—and then— (*his tone holds boyish amazement*) and then her singling out a poor fish like me !

CANON (*nodding his head thoughtfully*). I see.

SIMON. Kay and I felt it was no good hanging about. The sooner we got married the better. We felt Jackie would get over it quicker that way.

CANON. A very convenient belief. And did she ?

SIMON. She'd made certain threats, of course . . .

CANON (*sharply*). Threats ?

SIMON (*apologetically*). She's half French, you know. Latin blood. She talked a lot of melodramatic nonsense about shooting us both. I shouldn't really have been surprised at her taking a pot shot at me— but I'd never have believed she'd react in this way.

CANON. In what way ?

SIMON (*rising and moving up* LC). I'm telling this thing awfully badly. Kay and I started off on our honeymoon. Went to Venice. The first thing we saw when we got to Danielli's was Jackie sitting in the lounge. For a minute of two I was afraid of trouble—but she was quite polite. Just expressed surprise at seeing us, said what a coincidence it was. Naturally I thought it was a coincidence. Just a bit of bad luck. Anyway, Kay and I thought we'd push on, so we caught an earlier boat from Trieste. Dashed if when we got on board Jackie wasn't there. Seems *she* was going to Egypt, too. It was damned awkward, you know, sir. It really was. (*He comes down to the chair above the* C *table.*)

CANON. Yes, I can imagine that.

SIMON (*putting one foot on the chair*). Well, to come to the point, when we landed in Egypt we went to the Mena House near Cairo. Jackie had said she was going up to Luxor. But when we came down to dinner the first night—Jackie was there.

CANON. Very unusual—yes, and ingenious.

SIMON. I must admit I absolutely saw red. Afterwards I went up and tackled her, accused her of following us round. She was as cool as a cucumber, just smiled sweetly and said it was odd that we always seemed to choose the same places! I told her it had got to stop.

CANON. And what had she to say to that?

SIMON. She said, "But surely there's no law against my stopping in the same hotel as you and Kay?" And, of course, she had me there. Kay kept saying that we must take steps of some kind—but I don't really see that there are any steps one can take.

CANON. You told me just now that both you and Jacqueline were as poor as church mice. How then does she manage to meet the expenses of travel? They must be heavy.

SIMON (*with admiration*). That's clever of you. Do you know, I never thought of that. Jackie's poor as they make them, the time's bound to come when she'll run out. She's only got about two hundred a year.

CANON. Then presumably she will soon come to the end of her resources and be penniless.

(SIMON *looks uncomfortable. He crosses to* RC.)
You don't like to think of that?

SIMON. Well, *I* can't help it. It's not my fault. If she will start on this crackbrained scheme—can't she see what an ass she's making of herself? Hasn't she got any pride—any dignity?

CANON. Pride and dignity are qualities we are always apt to urge on other people.

SIMON. What does she expect to get out of following me round and making an exhibition of herself?

CANON. It has already caused you and Kay a good deal of annoyance and vexation, has it not?

SIMON. It's got Kay absolutely on the raw. That's why—(*He stops abruptly.*)

CANON. Yes?

SIMON (*coming above the* C *table*). She followed us to Luxor. When we got to Assouan she was there again. Kay just couldn't stand any more. So we hitched up a scheme. Gave out that we were going down to Cairo again by steamer to-morrow. Then to-day we started off on a day's expedition to Philae. In the meantime Louise, Kay's maid, sneaked quietly out of the hotel with the luggage and drove to this boat ready for us. It won't be until this evening after dinner that Jackie will discover we've gone—and by then this boat will have started. We've bribed the porter to tell Jackie that we've gone back by train to Cairo.

CANON. Very elaborate.

SIMON. So, you see, there won't be a thing she can do about it. Even if she finds out where we've really gone, she can only come after us by the next boat. Kay's idea is to fly from Khartoum down to East Africa, or even to the Cape.

CANON (*eyeing him keenly*). You like this scheme?

SIMON (*crossing down* L; *breaking out*). No, I don't. After all, it's neither more nor less than running away. And that sticks in my gizzard, I'm all for standing firm and seeing it out. I don't like the idea of running away from a girl. I feel a coward. But Kay . . .

CANON. Kay?

SIMON (*slowly*). Kay's nerves are all shot to pieces. She feels she must get away. (*He pauses.*) I'm glad I've told you all this, sir—glad we came across you. I don't suppose you think much of me. I know I'm not nearly good enough for Kay. But I do love her—and I'll always do every mortal thing she wants.

CANON. Tcha, tcha, you mustn't do that sort of thing, young man. Kay has always had her own way far too much. You must stand up to her.

(KAY *enters* R. *She is in holiday mood. She has changed.*)

KAY. Well, here I am. Got a drink for me? (*She crosses to* C *above the table.* SIMON *presses the bell by the window down* L.) Have you persuaded Uncle Ambrose that you're the right husband for me?

SIMON. He says I ought to beat you.

KAY (*to* CANON PENNEFATHER). How discerning of you. (*She turns to the window and looks out at the view.*) Oh dear, what fun this is going to be!

CANON. The sunsets here are wonderful.

KAY. There's hardly anybody on board. Late in the season, of course. We shall practically have the boat to ourselves. We can do just what we like.

CANON. That will be no novelty to you, Kay.

(*The* STEWARD *enters* L.)

SIMON (*to* KAY). What will you drink?

KAY. Sherry.

SIMON (*to the* STEWARD). A sherry and two gin-fizzes.

CANON. Oh, I don't think I . . .

SIMON. Oh, yes, do, sir!

CANON. Well, perhaps this once.

SIMON (*to the* STEWARD). Sherry and two gin-fizzes.

(*The* STEWARD *exits* L.)

CANON. By the way, Kay, I'd like a thousand pounds.

SIMON. A thousand pounds?

CANON (*cheerfully*). Conscience money.

KAY. Don't look so surprised, darling. Uncle Ambrose always does this sort of thing. He's a kind of moral gangster. (*She comes down to the chair above the table.*)

SIMON. I don't understand.

CANON. Kay has far more money than is good for her. A great many people have far too little for their good. I endeavour to readjust the balance. Blank cheque form.

(KAY *sits above the table.*)

I never ask for alms—I demand them ! I find it far more successful. (*He hands a fountain pen to* KAY.) Pen. Your rich man or woman signs a cheque and then goes out to lunch at the Berkeley with an inner glow that assists digestion. (*To* KAY.) Don't forget to put the branch of the bank. (*To* SIMON.) They have the comfortable feeling that they have reserved a front stall in Heaven.

KAY. You really are the most cynical clergyman I know. You don't even say thank you.

CANON. Why should I ? I am merely assisting you to make a good investment.

(*The* STEWARD *enters* L *with drinks. He crosses down stage to* CANON PENNEFATHER.)

STEWARD. In one or two minutes we start now. (*As he moves round the table to* KAY ; *he waves his hand.*) Scenery very fine !

(*He crosses to* SIMON *and then exits.* KAY *gives a sigh of relief and lifts her glass.*)

KAY. Here's to our trip !

(*They drink.*)

CANON. Come now, Kay. Sign, please.

KAY (*taking her cheque book out of her bag; objecting, but not very much*). A thousand pounds is a lot of money.

(SIMON *sits on the table down* L.)

CANON. It won't do very much, but it will do something.

KAY (*to* SIMON). Uncle Ambrose has some wonderful scheme for rebuilding a new England—self-supporting communities and industries—a kind of Christianised Soviet it seems to me. (*She writes the cheque.*)

CANON. You understand nothing about it, my dear, because you're not interested. But you have your place in the scheme. The lowest place—supplying funds.

KAY. I don't see how you ever get any money at all when you're so rude.

CANON. That, my child, shows that you have a very poor idea of psychology. (*He looks at the cheque.*) Five hundred pounds !

KAY. Fifty per cent of what you've asked for is pretty good going !

CANON (*taking the cheque and raising his glass*). Ah, well ! All's grist to the mill ! To Jerusalem !

KAY (*surprised*). Jerusalem ? (*She puts away the cheque book and hands back the pen.*)

CANON (*quoting; for the first time his urbane manner slips—a trace of fanaticism is seen*). "For I will build Jerusalem in England's green and pleasant land."

SIMON. Oh, dear !

KAY (*rising and crossing to* SIMON). Don't look so surprised, darling. It's only Uncle Ambrose on his hobby horse again !

(JACQUELINE DE SEVERAC *enters* R. *She is cool, composed, and looks quietly amused with life, yet betrays consciousness that her entrance is dramatic.*)

JACKIE (*betraying slightly exaggerated surprise*). Hullo, Kay, how surprising! I thought you and Simon were going down river to Cairo. I never expected to find you here.

KAY (*absolutely taken back*). I—you didn't—(*She moves above the table down* L.)

(SIMON *springs up, his face black with rage.*)

SIMON (*crossing to* C *below the table*). Look here, Jackie—(*He stops.*)

JACKIE (*sweetly*). Yes, Simon? How hot you look. It is hot, isn't it?

KAY. Yes—it's the glass here—makes it very hot, I think. (*She sits at the table down* L.)

(SIMON *crosses to* JACKIE, *seemingly forgetting* CANON PENNEFATHER, *who watches with great interest.*)

SIMON. So you're still playing this game, are you?

JACKIE. I don't know what you mean. I thought the trip up to the second cataract sounded so interesting.

SIMON. Oh, cut it out, Jackie!

JACKIE. But surely, Simon, you and Kay were going to Cairo to-morrow? Everybody in the hotel was saying so.

SIMON. Sometimes one alters one's plans.

JACKIE. Yes. I altered mine.

SIMON. You can't go on doing this sort of thing, you know! It's—it's so—so utterly unreasonable!

JACKIE. What *are* you talking about, Simon? (*She looks about and crosses up stage to* LC.) This seems a nice boat. I shall enjoy this trip to Wadi Halfa. (*To* KAY.) Especially now that I've found friends on board. I must find out where my cabin is.

(*The* STEWARD *enters* R.)

STEWARD. Miss de Severac? Welcome to *Lotus*. This way, please.

(JACKIE *crosses and exits* R *accompanied by the* STEWARD.)

KAY (*rising*). There's still time, Simon. We could get off—

SIMON. And if we did—she'd only follow us. I wish I could make you see that running away only plays into her hands. We've got to go through with it—beat her at her own game. Otherwise she sees she's got us rattled, and that spurs her on.

KAY. Yes—yes, that's true. (*She thinks a minute, then looks at* CANON PENNEFATHER. *She crosses to* SIMON *and gives him a little authoritative push.*) Go away, darling—go to the cabin—or to the deck lounge the other end of the boat. I want to talk to Uncle Ambrose.

SIMON. He knows all about it. I've told him.

KAY (*urging him to the door* R). Good. Then that will save time. Go on, darling. You'll cramp my style.

(SIMON *goes rather unwillingly out* R.)

(*She brings the chair from up* R *down to* R *of* CANON PENNEFATHER. *She looks determined.*) Uncle Ambrose, you've got to help me.

CANON. In what way?

KAY. Simon's told you all about this—this incredible persecution. Jackie is making herself utterly ridiculous. But all the same, it's got to be stopped. You've got to stop it.

CANON (*raising his eyebrows*). Indeed? How do you suggest I should go about it?

KAY. Talk to her. Show her what a fool she is making of herself. Threaten her. Tell her that we shall take proceedings.

CANON. She's a perfect right to travel on this boat, Kay.

KAY. Well, appeal to her. Appeal to her pride and her self-respect. Show her how undignified it is to go on running after a man who doesn't want her.

CANON. Have you any reason to believe she would listen to me?

KAY. People do listen to you. You've got something about you that makes them listen.

CANON. I am to appeal, am I, to her better nature?

KAY. Yes. Get her to give up this silly persecution.

CANON. Why do you mind so much, Kay?

KAY (*rising and crossing down* LC). Wouldn't anybody? It's maddening. I simply can't stand it.

CANON. But you will have to stand it, won't you?

KAY. What do you mean?

CANON. That there isn't any way out. You can bear this thing well, or you can bear it badly—but you can't refuse to bear a thing that exists and that you cannot alter.

KAY. When we get to Wadi Halfa I'll charter an aeroplane. We'll fly right off into the wilds—

CANON. Fugitives!

(KAY *is silent, uneasy.*)

Come and sit down, Kay.

(KAY *sits* L *of the* C *table.*)

What are you running away from?

KAY. But you know!

CANON. Oh, yes, *I* know. I'm waiting for you to face facts.

KAY. I haven't the least idea of what you mean.

CANON. Haven't you? I'll ask my question again. *Why do you mind so much?*

KAY. Because it's—intolerable!

CANON. Quite. And yet there are other ways of looking at it. You might feel just annoyed. Or you might feel pity that a friend whom you loved should have been so deeply hurt as to cast all conventions aside. But instead this business has got right under your skin—(*He pauses, rises, and moves above the table. He stands over* KAY.) It's yourself you're running away from, Kay. You've had a happy life. You've been generous and kindly and you've always had good reason to think well of yourself. Naturally you don't like to feel guilty.

KAY (*angrily*). What do you mean by guilty?

CANON (*quoting*). "And the Lord sent Nathan unto David. And he came unto him and said unto him, 'There were two men in one city, the one rich and the other poor. The rich man had exceeding many flocks and herds, but the poor man had nothing save one little ewe lamb. (*He pauses.*) And the rich man took the poor man's ewe lamb.' "

KAY. It wasn't like that at all!

CANON. "And David said to Nathan, 'As the Lord liveth, the man that has done this is worthy to die . . . because he did this thing and because he had no pity.' And Nathan said to David, 'Thou art the man.' "

KAY. It wasn't like that, I tell you. Simon and Jackie weren't the least bit suited to each other. He realised that as soon as he met me. What on earth do you think he ought to have done? Gone on with it? Made three lives miserable? He couldn't have made Jackie happy if he wasn't happy himself.

CANON (*moving above the table and replacing the chair up* R). That is always assumed. A convenient assumption!

KAY. Surely it's better to rectify a mistake before it's too late? The only commonsense thing to do was for Simon to tell Jackie the truth. You'd think if she was so fond of him she'd want to put *his* happiness first.

CANON (*turning to her*). How very young you are, Kay!

KAY. Well, what's wrong with that?

CANON (*coming down* RC). Nothing. You were very fond of Jackie always, weren't you?

KAY. Yes, she was my greatest friend at school. I was devoted to her always.

CANON. And she to you?

KAY. Yes.

CANON. And she came to you and asked you to help her—to give the man she loved a job, so that they could marry?

KAY. Yes.

CANON (*moving below the table to* KAY). You've always had everything you wanted, haven't you, Kay? There's never been any reason why you shouldn't have it. But there was a reason this time.

KAY (*rising*). What are you trying to say? (*She turns up* LC.) You're blaming me for everything?

CANON (*following her*). I'm saying that there was a moment, right at the beginning, when you could have stopped. You saw Simon Mostyn and he attracted you. He was dazzled by you. But you could have held your hand, Kay. You could have said to yourself, "He's Jackie's man and I am Jackie's friend." You'd got everything—your friend's life was bound up in one person. But Kay had to have what she wanted. Like King David, you stretched out your hand and took the poor man's one ewe lamb.

KAY. You're dreadfully unfair!

CANON. Simon Mostyn is a weak man—one can see that. I think the initiative came from you.

KAY (*crossing to* RC). Well, what does all that matter *now*? One can't go back. The past is the past.

CANON. Exactly. The past conditions the future.

KAY (*turning*). Well then, what am I going to do about all this ?

CANON (*moving to* C). My dear child, I don't see that there is anything you can do.

KAY. You mean I'll have to put up with it ?

CANON. It seems so.

KAY. And you wont help me ?

CANON. I'm not very sure that I want to help you, Kay. It is some-one else I should like to be able to help.

KAY (*moving down* R). Oh, I don't understand your attitude.

CANON. Just one question, Kay, as a matter of curiosity. Why, since you are running away—

(KAY *makes a protest.*)

(*He raises his voice and repeats.*)—running away, why did you not hire a private dahabeah ?   Jacqueline could not have followed you on to that ?

KAY. Of course I thought of that.   I'm not a perfect idiot.   But it's Simon.   You've no idea of the trouble I've had.   He makes the most extraordinarily heavy weather just because I'm the one who has the money.   As though it mattered which of us has it !

CANON. Oh, but it does matter, Kay, from a man's point of view.

KAY. Well, anyway—Simon has been very difficult.   He hates the idea of what he calls living on me.   The only thing that would appease him at all was that at any rate the honeymoon should be what he calls "his show."   So I gave in, and he hasn't let me spend a penny.   He'd got shares or something, that he sold out, and the poor sweet has been so happy about it that I haven't had the heart to protest.   But a private dahabeah would be quite out of the question for him to pay for—and I simply didn't dare suggest that *I* should.

CANON. I must say I think a good deal better of your Simon for taking that stand.

KAY. Well, I think it's very stupid.   As if money mattered.

CANON. Naturally it doesn't to you—you've always had plenty of it.

KAY. Why are you so against me ?   I think you're most unkind !

(*She exits* R.   CANON PENNEFATHER *sits* R *of the table up* L, *shaking his head.*   SMITH *enters* L.   *He strolls about whistling.   He steals a few glances at* CANON PENNEFATHER.)

SMITH. Bit of a change from the King David Hotel—eh ?

CANON. Possibly.

SMITH. I expect you did yourself pretty well there amongst the fleshpots. (*He is down* RC.)

CANON. I ?

SMITH (*moving up* RC *to* C). I noticed you there.   Perhaps it was your double . . . sitting by one of those pillar things—(*significantly*)—opening a great wad of mail.

(CANON PENNEFATHER *looks at him.   There is a sense of conflict.*)

CANON. You seem to be a very observant young man.

SMITH. I usually recognise a face—and a figure.

CANON. Touché!

SMITH. Perhaps you don't understand what I'm getting at?

CANON. Oh, perfectly—you make your meaning quite plain.

SMITH. You parsons are all the same. I've no use for you.

CANON. You young men are all the same, but we have got a use for you.

SMITH. Well—I must admit you've got a nerve. Phew! It's too hot in here . . .

(He goes out R. *The call to prayer from the Minaret starts.* CANON PENNEFATHER *listens, then rises and goes to the window up* C. *After a minute or two* JACKIE *enters* L.)

CANON. We shall be starting in a minute or two. Ahead of us is what the old Egyptians called the hidden horizon.

JACKIE *(thoughtfully)*. Hidden horizon . . .

CANON. There is something I would like to say to you, Miss de Severac.

JACKIE. I'm sure there is. *(She sits at the table up* L.) Let's get on with it. I know who you are, of course. Kay has often talked of you. You are supposed to have the gift of eloquence. *(She pauses.)* Go on, I'm waiting. Will I be a good girl and leave dear persecuted Kay alone? That's it, isn't it?

CANON. I would put it differently.

JACKIE. I'm sure you would. It wouldn't be as crude as that.

CANON. Do you think you know what I am going to say?

JACKIE. I'm sure of it.

(The call to prayer ends.)

CANON. I wonder. Well, what I've got to say to you is this—*(with force)*—bury your dead!

JACKIE *(startled)*. What?

CANON *(coming down to the chair* L *of the* C *table and sitting, facing* L). Bury your dead. Give up the past. Turn to the future. What is done cannot be undone, and bitterness will certainly not undo it. You are young. Time will heal you.

JACKIE *(smiling)*. You're quite wrong. I'm not suffering. *(Quietly.)* I'm enjoying myself. Did you see their faces when I walked in this evening? *(Quietly.)* Oh yes, I'm enjoying myself.

CANON *(rising and crossing down* RC). That is the worst part of it.

JACKIE. You're rather harsh, aren't you, about my little amusements —but then, of course, they upset dear Kay. So I must give them up!

CANON. I'm not thinking about Kay. What you are doing won't do Kay any harm. She will just have to put up with it. The harm you are doing will be to yourself.

JACKIE. To my soul?

CANON. You're afraid of the word? I'm not. You've still got a few minutes. Get off this boat. Make a new life for yourself.

JACKIE *(rising)*. You don't understand. Simon is my life. We loved each other.

CANON. I know how much you cared for him.

JACKIE (*moving up* LC). We loved each other. I tell you. And I trusted Kay. She was my best friend. I'd never even been jealous of all she had and I hadn't. All her life Kay has been able to buy everything she wanted. She's never denied herself anything. When she saw Simon she wanted him and she just—took him!

CANON. And he allowed himself to be—bought?

JACKIE. No, that's not true. He didn't marry Kay for her money—but there's such a thing as the glamour money gives. Kay has an atmosphere. Do you wonder it went to his head? (*She moves to the window up* C *and makes a gesture outside.*) Look out there. Soon the moon will be up—quite plain to see. But when the sun shines you can't see the moon. I was the moon. When the sun came out Simon couldn't see me any more. He was dazzled. He could only see the sun—Kay.

CANON. So that is how you see it? (*He moves a few steps up* RC.)

JACKIE. Glamour. She went to his head. There's her complete assurance, too, her habit of command. She's so sure of herself that she makes other people sure. Simon was weak, perhaps, but then he's a very simple person. (*She moves down* LC.) He would have loved me and me only if Kay hadn't come along.

CANON. That is what you like to think.

JACKIE. It's true. He did love me—he always will love me.

CANON. Does he love you now?

(JACKIE *starts. Her face changes. She speaks bitterly.*)

JACKIE. One up to you on that. (*She moves away to* L.) You don't hit softly, do you?

CANON. I'm afraid for you.

JACKIE. Afraid?

CANON. Yes. What you are doing is dangerous.

JACKIE. Not as dangerous as what I once thought of doing. Do you know what I felt when it first happened? (*She takes a small pistol out of her bag; crosses to him and shows it.*)

CANON (*taking it and reading the initials*). J.S.

JACKIE. Nice little thing. Looks like a toy, but a bullet from it would kill a man or woman. And I'm a good shot. (*She takes back the pistol and weighs it in her hand.*) I meant to kill one or other of them. Not both—that wouldn't have been satisfactory. If I'd thought Kay would have looked afraid—but she wouldn't. She's got plenty of physical courage. And then I thought I'd wait. After all, I could do it any time —it would be more fun to wait—and think about it—(*Her face changes as she pauses and visualises revenge.*) And then this idea came to my mind— to follow them. (*She moves up* RC *to up* C.) Whenever they arrived at some far away spot and were together and happy, they should see *me*! And it worked. It got Kay badly—in a way nothing else could have done. That was when I began to enjoy myself . . . (*As she comes down to the chair* L *of the* C *table.*) And there's nothing she can do about it! I'm always perfectly pleasant and polite. And it's poisoning everything —everything for them . . . (*She sits and laughs hysterically.*)

(CANON PENNEFATHER *crosses swiftly above the table to her and catches her by the wrist.*)

CANON. Be quiet—quiet, I tell you !
JACKIE. Why should I ? (*But she stops.*)
CANON. Because that is how the devils in Hell laugh.
JACKIE. I'm in Hell all right.
CANON (*sitting* C *above the table*). Listen Jacqueline, don't open your heart to evil, because if you do—evil will come.
JACKIE. Isn't evil rather a strong word ?
CANON. It is the only word.
JACKIE. You can't stop me.
CANON. No, I cannot stop you.
JACKIE. Even if I were to kill her, you couldn't stop me.
CANON (*with deep sadness*). No.
JACKIE. Is it so wrong to kill a person who has taken away everything you had in the world ? Is it ? Is it ?
CANON. Yes !

(JACKIE *looks at him, then laughs—the tension slackens. She speaks mockingly.*)

JACKIE. You ought to approve of my present scheme of revenge, because as long as it works, I shan't use that pistol. But I'm afraid sometimes.
CANON. What are you afraid of ?
JACKIE. Sometimes—everything goes red—I want to hurt her. (*Carried away.*) I want to stick a knife into her. I want to put my dear little pistol close against her head . . . (*gesture follows words*) and then just press that trigger—so—

(*The sounds of anchor chains and Arab voices are heard.*)

CANON. We are casting off. For the last time, I beg of you—not because of Kay's peace of mind, but for your own lasting peace, and your future happiness—get off this boat ! Give up this journey !
JACKIE. I almost wish I could. (*She speaks with deep weariness.*)
CANON. But you can. There is always a moment when one can turn back—before it is too late. This is *your* moment.

(*The sound of paddles turning is heard. The* STEWARD *steps inside the door* L *looking ashore.* CANON PENNEFATHER *rises and goes up* C.)

STEWARD. We start now. Bismillah er-rahman er-ranim !

(*He looks at them, smiles, and goes out* R.)

JACKIE. What was that he said ?
CANON. What most Mahommedans say before starting out on a journey. In the name of Allah—(*meaningly*) the Compassionate, the Merciful. Can *you* say that on the start of your journey ?

JACKIE (*rising*). I wish you hadn't been on board! (*She takes a step* L.)

(KAY *enters* R.)

KAY. I can't stand any more of it.

(SIMON *enters* R.)

SIMON. No, Kay, we've got to go through with it.
JACKIE (*her face changing*). Yes! We've got to go through with it!

CURTAIN.

ACT II.

SCENE 1.

SCENE.—*The same. Three days later. By the temple of Abu Simbel.*

It is evening, after dinner. The lights are lit; the windows are closed but not curtained. It is bright moonlight outside.

When the CURTAIN *rises* CANON PENNEFATHER, MISS FFOLIOT-FFOULKES, SIMON, *and* KAY *are at the* C *table playing bridge. They are seated respectively above, below,* L *and* R *of the table.*

The STEWARD *enters as they play a couple of tricks, and sprays all round with a Flit spray. Jackals can be heard howling, also occasional shots and Arab singing throughout the scene.*

CANON. And the rest are mine. (*He puts down his hand.*) Game and rubber.

(*The* STEWARD *exits.*)

KAY (*to* SIMON). Do you mean to say we had all the hearts between us? Why didn't you lead them?

SIMON. I only had ace, queen, and another.

KAY. I had five to the king—and not another card in my hand. (*She rises and moves behind* CANON PENNEFATHER.) Uncle Ambrose, you wicked old man, as soon as you got in with the ace of diamonds, you actually *led* the knave of hearts. How many had you?

CANON (*chuckling*). Knave singleton. I had to frighten you off the heart suit. I should have been heavily down if you'd led one.

SIMON. Poker ought to be your game, sir.

KAY. He's got a regular poker face.

MISS FFOLIOT-FFOULKES. Dear Canon Pennefather. I think we can congratulate ourselves on our tactics. (*Referring to the score.*) I think that makes us nine hundred points?

CANON. Seven hundred, I think.

SIMON. In spite of your poker face, most honourable over the score! I'm awfully slack. I never add up. I always trust to my opponents. (SIMON *pays.*)

KAY (*crossing to the table down* L). You're dreadfully lazy, Simon. (*Yawns.*) I usually keep the score—but I'm so terribly sleepy tonight. (*She picks up a book.*) Oh dear, I *must* go to bed! Simon, pay for me. (*She crosses down stage towards* R.)

SIMON. It's the sightseeing that has tired you.

KAY. Abu Simbel is wonderful, though. I wouldn't have missed it for anything. I feel we ought really to have gone again this evening with the others and seen it by artificial light. The dragoman said one could see far more details of the wall paintings.

MISS FFOLIOT-FFOULKES. Sometimes, my dear Mrs. Mostyn, the details are not—well—quite *nice*. And I find dragomen are often so insistent on—er—certain aspects of the Egyptian mythology and customs.

CANON. Indeed ? I have always found dragomen the soul of delicacy —quite disappointingly so.

(KAY *sits in the chair down* R.)

MISS FFOLIOT-FFOULKES. That, dear Canon, shows the purity of your own mind. (*She looks round and rises.*) Now where is my velvet scarf ? Christina! Where is Christina? Oh, of course, she has gone ashore. Most inconsiderate. How did she know what I might want or not want during the evening ? Always thinking of *pleasure*—these young people !

(CANON PENNEFATHER *rises and searches up* L.)

Oh, thank you, dear Canon, pray do not trouble—I had it before dinner, I know. I was sitting here. (*She goes to the table up* R.)   I can't think.

(SIMON *rises and searches down* L.)

—Oh, thank you, Mr. Mostyn, pray don't trouble—velvet—purple velvet.

(SIMON *sits again and plays patience.*)

Dear, dear, where can my scarf be? Most annoying of Christina not to have looked after it properly. Don't you find, Canon, that young people nowadays have absolutely no consideration for their elders ?
CANON. Sometimes. And sometimes their elders have very little consideration for them. (*He comes to the chair above the* C *table.*)

(*Noises are heard from off* L.)

I think I hear the party returning.
MISS FFOLIOT-FFOULKES. Christina should have stayed quietly on board with me. Especially since that dreadful socialistic young man was to be of the party. So terribly common. And so pushing.

(DR. BESSNER *and* JACKIE *enter* L.)

CANON. And what was the temple like by moonlight ?

(JACKIE *moves up* C.)

DR. BESSNER (*crossing to the table up* R). It was marvellous, quite different. The scenes on the walls of great interest are—the march of Egyptian army under Rameses to Kadesh on North Wall—also leading by the king before the Harakhte of many prisoners—while temple of course is dedicated to Ra Harakhte—and Amen Ra, God for Thebes.
CANON. Thank you, Herr Doktor !

(CHRISTINA *and* SMITH *enter* L.)

MISS FFOLIOT-FFOULKES. While *you* have been enjoying yourself, Christina, *I* have been put to serious inconvenience. Where is my purple scarf ?

CHRISTINA (*coming down* LC). You had it before dinner, Aunt Helen, in here.

(SMITH *sits on the table up* L.)

MISS FFOLIOT-FFOULKES. Well, it isn't here now.

CHRISTINA. Maybe it's in your cabin.

MISS FFOLIOT-FFOULKES. I am not aware that scarves have legs. I brought it in *here*.

CHRISTINA. The steward may have taken it there while you were down at dinner. I'll go and see. (*She crosses down stage to* RC.)

MISS FFOLIOT-FFOULKES. Don't rush off like that. (*She turns to the bridge table.*) Take my knitting . . . and my glasses . . . and my little shawl. There is no reason why I should have to carry *everything* myself.

(CHRISTINA *takes the glasses and shawl from the table* C.)

SMITH. That's what I always say. If you own a dogsbody, keep it on the run.

(CHRISTINA *crosses towards the table up* L.)

MISS FFOLIOT-FFOULKES (*freezingly to* SMITH). Perhaps you wouldn't mind getting off my knitting.

SMITH. Sorry. (*He gets off the table.*).

(CHRISTINA *takes the knitting and crosses towards the door* R.)

MISS FFOLIOT-FFOULKES. Social embarrassment makes people so clumsy with their—er—er . . .

(*She goes off* R *with* CHRISTINA.)

SMITH. Bullying old b . . . harridan.

KAY (*getting up and yawning*). I must go to bed.

CANON. One moment, Kay, you said you would sign those transfers this evening. I've got them here.

KAY. Oh, darling, can't they wait until to-morrow morning ?

CANON. This morning you said they could wait until to-night ! It won't take a minute, and I must get them off from Wadi Halfa.

(*He picks up the portfolio from beside the chair above the* C *table, opens it and sets some documents in front of* KAY. *He opens them at the place to be signed.* KAY *sits* R *of the* C *table.* CANON PENNEFATHER *gives her a fountain pen.* SIMON *rises and crosses behind* KAY. *He stands looking over her shoulder.* KAY, *still yawning, turns the papers back to the first page and begins to read them through.*)

SIMON. You're not going to read the whole thing through, are you.?

KAY. I always read everything before signing it. Father taught me to. He said one never knew if some clerical error mightn't have crept in.

SMITH. Clerical error ! That's good.

CANON. Kay is an excellent woman of business.

SIMON. Well, I've never read through a legal document in my life. (*He laughs.*) Wouldn't understand it if I did. I just sign on the dotted line as I'm told.

CANON (*looking at him thoughtfully*). Indeed.

SIMON. Well, you can't go through the world thinking everybody is going to do you down. I've always found it pays to trust people.

KAY. Father never trusted anybody. Uncle Ambrose was the only man he believed in—that's why he left him my guardian and trustee of my capital until I was twenty-five or married. Father said lawyers knew too much about how to evade the law.

CANON. Melhuish Ridgeway was a very shrewd and able man.

(DR. BESSNER *starts at the name, and sits at the table up* R *and stares at* KAY.)

He was a great master of finance—but he had little belief in his fellow men.

SMITH. Perhaps rightly.

CANON. On the other hand he little knew the subterfuges to which some of the clergy will descend to get money for their pet causes.

KAY. I suppose I've actually come into my capital now, Uncle Ambrose. (*She laughs.*) I could make a will and leave it all to your Better and Brighter England scheme.

CANON. You could. But I'm quite sure you will not be induced to invest your money in that excellent fashion.

KAY. Why not ?

CANON. Because the dividends, my dear, are not payable in this world.

KAY. I wonder what it would feel like to be really poor—

SIMON. Don't worry ; (*with a trace of bitterness*) you'll never know.

SMITH. Are you all so sure of that ? (*He comes down* L.) The patience of the workers won't last for ever. (*He sits at the table down* L.)

KAY. Oh, don't let's be political. (*She yawns.*)

CANON. Yes, I think, my dear, that these *had* better wait until the morning. (*He takes the papers away.*)

KAY. I simply can't take in anything. (*She gets up and kisses* CANON PENNEFATHER.) Good night, Uncle Ambrose. It's been a lovely day. (*In a low voice to him.*) You were right about facing things —I've got over my silly attack of nerves. (*She moves up* C *towards* JACKIE, *pauses, and speaks with affection.*) Good night, Jackie. (*Pause.*) It's really rather heavenly on this boat, isn't it ?

(JACKIE *does not answer.* SIMON *moves to the door* R *and opens it.* KAY *hesitates, then exits* R.)

CANON (*moving up* C). Good night, Jacqueline.

(JACKIE *is staring after* KAY. CANON PENNEFATHER *stands waiting. She suddenly realises he is waiting for her to speak. She looks up at him fiercely, and speaks in a low tense voice.*)

JACKIE. She doesn't care any more. Neither of them cares—I can't reach them . . . They've got beyond me. They don't mind if I'm here or not . . . I can't . . . I can't hurt them any more . . .

CANON. Do you still want to hurt them ?
JACKIE. They shan't be happy together—they shan't ! They shan't ! . . . I'll stop it somehow !
CANON. You should not have come on this boat.
JACKIE (*her voice suddenly weary*). You're right . . . yes, I think you're right . . . But it's too late now . . . I can't go back. I've got to go on . . . to go on . . . (*Her hands clench.*)
CANON (*gently*). You are very tired. It has been a long hot day. Go to bed and sleep.
JACKIE. I couldn't sleep . . . (*She breaks towards the door L.*)
CANON. Oh yes, you could. (*He follows her.*)
JACKIE. No—it's too hot—too still. It's the kind of evening when things snap !

(CANON PENNEFATHER *shakes his head gently, then sighs and goes out L.*)

(*Calling.*) Boy !

(SIMON *picks up a magazine, moves to the chair* R *of the* C *table and sits. The* STEWARD *appears at* L.)

JACKIE. Bring me a double brandy. (*She moves up* C *and looks out of the window.*)

(SIMON *gives a quick look at her. The* STEWARD *goes.*)

DR. BESSNER (*coming to the chair above the* C *table*). You will excuse me, please, but is your wife then the daughter of Melhuish Ridgeway ?

(SMITH *is interested.* JACKIE *begins to hum* "Frankie and Johnnie" *under her breath.*)

SIMON. Yes.
DR. BESSNER. I did not know that.
SIMON. Is there any reason why you should know it ?
DR. BESSNER (*showing emotion*). You will excuse me . . . you see . . . that man—that man . . . (*He sits above the* C *table.*)
SMITH. Am I right in thinking that one of Melhuish Ridgeway's financial operations has at some time affected you personally ?

(*The* STEWARD *enters* L *with drink. He crosses up* C. JACKIE *takes the drink and sits at the table up* R. *She pays no attention to the others and sits staring straight ahead. Her humming grows louder.*)

DR. BESSNER. You will forgive me, gentlemen—but I have very strong feelings. (*Much affected.*) In my country in Europe—a small country—an obscure country—that man, he buys the politicians—he corrupts the government. Those who get the concession, you understand—it is not that they want to develop it—on the contrary—the people—the peasants—they starve. The ore, you see, it would be a rival and that must not be—instead, all is desolate—deserted. (*He gesticulates.*) And we who believed in it, we lose all we had ! We are finished, wiped out. My father, an old man and feeble, he dies with the heart broken. But it is not the non-progress—the industry that not developed is—the—the ah, you understand ?

SMITH. Frankly, old boy, no. But I get the general idea. International finance, like some obscene spider, up to its usual tricks. And old man Ridgeway, sitting in his office in London with a big cigar, right in the centre of the web. No offence, Mostyn, but Melhuish Ridgeway's methods are pretty common knowledge and his handsome donations to charities can't quite wipe out the taste of them.

SIMON. Oh, that's all right by me. I never even saw my father-in-law. He was dead years before I met Kay. I suppose these financial birds usually sail fairly near the wind. Don't know anything about finance myself. Often wish I did.

DR. BESSNER (*still very emotional*). The little man in the back street, he would be sent to prison—but the big man with the cigar, he can rob and cheat and stay inside the law.

SMITH. It won't be so for ever.

(CHRISTINA *enters* R.)

DR. BESSNER. They, too, should suffer—yes, suffer. Forgive me, I am upset.

(*He rises and hurries off* L.)

CHRISTINA (*looking accusingly at* SMITH). What have you been saying to upset poor Dr. Bessner ?

(*She crosses down stage to him.*)

SMITH. Me ? I like that ! Nothing at all. And why should you defend him ?

CHRISTINA. He's a foreigner. And foreigners are very sensitive. Their feelings are easily hurt.

SMITH (*rising*). And what about my feelings ? Your aunt taunted me this evening with my inferior social position.

CHRISTINA. You must forgive Aunt Helen. It's been a tiring day for her and the dust and sand affect her eyes.

SMITH. "Darkness falls from the sky ; Dust hath closed Helen's eye"— I wish it would.

JACKIE. Boy !

(*The* STEWARD *enters* L.)

Get me another brandy.

SMITH. And get me a pink gin. Christina ?

CHRISTINA. I wouldn't mind a lemonade. (*She sits* L *of the* C *table.*)

SMITH. Too tame ; make it a gin-fizz. What about you, Mostyn ?

SIMON. No, thanks.

(*The* STEWARD *exits* L.)

JACKIE (*singing*). "He was her man—and he done her wrong."

CHRISTINA (*to* JACKIE). It's a really 'lovely night—beautiful moonlight.

JACKIE. Yes, a real honeymoon night.

(SIMON *shifts uncomfortably, rises, and moves up* C *with a magazine.*)

CHRISTINA. The dragoman was telling me that one of the Egyptian goddesses—the one that's said to hold up the sky—was called Mutt. (*Thoughtfully.*) It seems an odd name for a goddess.

JACKIE. Why? She is a mutt to hold up the sky. Let it crash.

(*There is a pause. The* STEWARD *enters* L *with the drinks.*)

(*She rises and comes to the table down* R. *She has left her handbag on the table up* R. *To* CHRISTINA.) Come and sit by me, Christina. We'll drink together. (*She sits down* R.)

(*The* STEWARD *comes down* L *of* CHRISTINA. CHRISTINA *takes her drink, rises, and crosses to the chair* R *of the* C *table.*)

CHRISTINA. I must be going to bed. It's getting late.

(SMITH *takes his drink from the* STEWARD.)

JACKIE. Nonsense. The night is yet young. I want you to tell me all about yourself.

(*The* STEWARD *crosses to* JACKIE.)

CHRISTINA. There's not much to tell. (*She sits.*)

JACKIE (*taking her drink*). Well, here's to crime. (*To the* STEWARD.) You can bring me another.

(*The* STEWARD *exits* L. SIMON *makes a faint movement of protest.* JACKIE *looks over at him and laughs.*)

SMITH (*sitting on the table down* L). Talking of crime, I feel something should be done about your aunt. A nice little dose of arsenic, for instance.

CHRISTINA. You're very rude about my aunt.

SMITH. You can't tell me you *like* the woman?

CHRISTINA. She's been very good to me—bringing me abroad and everything.

SMITH. Including treating you as a slave. Haven't you got any spirit?

(JACKIE *begins to sing "Frankie and Johnnie" again.*)

Don't you know you're just as good as she is?

CHRISTINA. Oh, but I'm not.

SMITH. All that you mean is that she's rich and you're poor.

CHRISTINA. Not at all. Aunt Helen's highly educated and very cultured . . .

SMITH. Pah! Culture! Education! They mean nothing at all.

CHRISTINA. You know, I believe it's your digestion that's wrong. Aunt Helen was once ordered a special kind of pepsin. Would you like me to get some of it for you to try? It might make you much better tempered, and better mannered.

SMITH. What's wrong with my manners?

CHRISTINA (*calmly*). They're just atrocious.

SMITH. In that case, I will wish you good night.

CHRISTINA. Good night. I'm going to bed myself. (*She rises and starts towards the door* R.)

(JACKIE *clutches* CHRISTINA *by the arm*.)

JACKIE (*a little drunk*).   You can't go to bed.   I won't let you go to bed.   I want someone to talk to.   (*She rises*.)   Sit here and tell me all about yourself.

(*The* STEWARD *enters* L *with a drink.   He crosses down* C.)

(*As she crosses* CHRISTINA *to the* STEWARD.)   Have another drink?

CHRISTINA.   No, thank you.

(*The* STEWARD *exits* L.   JACKIE *sings a couple of verses of* "*Frankie and Johnnie.*"   SMITH *picks up a magazine, looks at it, and saunters out* L.)

(*Uncomfortably*.)   Really, I think I'll go to bed.   I'm very tired.

JACKIE.   I forbid you to go to bed.   Tell me about your life.   Tell me all about your life.

CHRISTINA (*sitting at the table down* R).   There's not much to tell.

(JACKIE *sits* R *of the table* C.)

I've lived in Edinburgh all my life.   I've got one sister and two brothers. I work in an insurance office.   I'd always wanted to travel.   When Aunt Helen brought me on this trip I could hardly believe it at first.   It was like a dream coming true.   I'm just loving every minute of it.

JACKIE.   You're a happy sort of person, aren't you?   God, I'd like to be you!

CHRISTINA.   Oh, but I'm sure . . . I mean . . .

JACKIE.   What do you mean?   Shall I tell you the story of *my* life?

(SIMON *rustles the magazine*.)

(*She turns her head, looks at* SIMON, *and laughs*.)   Simon would rather I didn't.

(SIMON *comes down* L.)

Going to run away, Simon?

SIMON (*flushing and sitting at the table down* L).   It's getting late.

JACKIE.   Just the right time of night for telling hard luck stories. Or good luck stories like Christina's.   Why hasn't your Aunt Helen ever taken you abroad before?   Why does she let you slave away in an office?

CHRISTINA.   That's a family affair.   Aunt Helen's sister, you see, married, as Aunt Helen considered, beneath her.   That was my grandmother—Aunt Helen's my great aunt.   My father, who's a proud man, kept up the quarrel until recently . . .

JACKIE.   Quite romantic.   Isn't it, Simon?

(SIMON *doesn't answer*.)

(*To* CHRISTINA.)   I like you, Christina.   I like you very much.   Don't go away and leave me, will you?   I'm feeling very low to-night.   I want someone to talk to.   You won't leave me, will you?

CHRISTINA (*embarrassed*).   I'm thinking we all need some sleep.

JACKIE (*sings some more of* "*Frankie and Johnnie.*"   *Then, sharply*). Boy!   (*After a pause*.)   Boy!   (*To* SIMON.)   Get the steward, will you, SIMON?   I want another drink.

SIMON. The stewards have gone to bed. It's after midnight.

JACKIE. I tell you I want another drink.

SIMON. You've had quite enough drinks, Jackie.

JACKIE (*rising*). What damned business is it of yours ?

SIMON. None.

JACKIE (*watching him and laughing jeeringly*). What's the matter, Simon ? Are you afraid ?

(SIMON *rather elaborately rises and takes the magazine to the table up* L *and fetches another one. He returns to his chair with it and reads.*)

CHRISTINA (*half-rising*). I really must . . .

JACKIE (*stopping her*). No, you mustn't. Do you know what Simon over there is afraid of ? He's afraid I'm going to tell you the story of my life.

CHRISTINA (*embarrassed*). Oh, indeed ?

JACKIE. It's a very sad story . . . He and I were engaged, you see . . . (*She sings.*) "He was her man, and he did her wrong . . ." He treated me rather badly . . . didn't you, Simon ?

SIMON (*angrily*). Go to bed, Jackie, you're drunk.

JACKIE. If you're embarrassed, you'd better leave the room.

SIMON. I'm staying.

CHRISTINA (*rising*). I really . . . it's so late . . .

JACKIE (*holding her arm*). I forbid you to go. You're to stay and hear what I've got to say.

SIMON. Jackie, you're making a fool of yourself. For God's sake, go to bed.

(*The beat of the tom-toms can be heard coming from the shore.*)

JACKIE (*rapidly and venomously*). You're afraid of a scene, aren't you ? That's because you're so English, so reticent. (*She moves to the table up* R *and picks up her handbag.*) You want me to behave decently, don't you ? Decently—like a prep. school boy. That's all you are—a great overgrown schoolboy. You'd better get out of here quickly, because I'm going to talk a lot. You damned fool, do you think you can treat me as you have done and get away with it ?

(SIMON *rises and moves to* L *of the table* C. *He is about to speak, then thinks better of it, and sits in the chair* LC. *He turns the pages of his magazine.*)

(*She comes down* LC *below the* C *table ; screaming at* SIMON.) Answer me, can't you ? Answer me ! I told you that I'd kill you sooner than let you go to another woman. You don't think I meant that ? You're wrong. I've only been waiting. Just waiting. You're *my* man, do you hear ? You belong to me. (*She slips the pistol out of her handbag unseen by* CHRISTINA.)

(SIMON *still doesn't speak.*)

I told you I'd kill you and I meant it . . . Answer me . . . damn you . . . answer me !

SIMON. Stop making a damned fool of yourself and go to bed.

JACKIE. I'm making a fool of myself, am I?
SIMON. Yes.
JACKIE. I'll kill you . . . I'll kill you . . . I'll shoot you like a dog . . .
like the dirty dog you are— (*She turns on him with the pistol.*)

(SIMON *springs to his feet as* JACKIE *pulls trigger.* CHRISTINA *gives a muffled scream.* SIMON *falls back into the chair* L *of the* C *table. He takes a handkerchief from his pocket and clasps it to his knee. A red stain comes through.* JACKIE *stands as though paralysed—then she staggers towards the door* R *and lets the pistol fall from her hand. She shuffles slowly forward.* CHRISTINA *is about to run* L, *but* JACKIE *comes down* R *of her, catches her and holds on to her.* JACKIE *is wavering to and fro on her feet.*)

Simon—Simon—I didn't mean . . .

(SMITH *runs in from* L. *He comes to* L *of* SIMON.)

SMITH. Hullo, what's up? Did—

(*The* STEWARD *comes in* L.)

STEWARD. What happen—?
SIMON (*forcing a laugh and addressing the* STEWARD). Nothing—
nothing—just a bit of fun—joke—very funny—you understand—(*He laughs.*)

(*The* STEWARD *grins doubtfully.*)

Go away. Don't come back—understand? *Not come back.*

(*The* STEWARD *nods and goes out* L.)

SMITH. What did happen?
JACKIE (*moving to the chair above the* C *table and sitting; hysterically*).
I shot him. Oh, God, I shot him.
CHRISTINA (*moving to* R *of* JACKIE). Hush, dear, hush . . .
SIMON (*to* SMITH). Get her away. For God's sake, get her out of
here. We've got to keep this quiet, you understand?

(SMITH *nods and crosses behind* SIMON *to* L *of* JACKIE.)

Get her outside. Then go and knock up Bessner. Make him give her
some dope or something to quieten her down, then bring him along here.
SMITH. Right.
JACKIE. Oh, Simon, Simon . . . (*She sobs.*) I'll kill myself.
SIMON (*to* CHRISTINA). Don't leave her.
SMITH (*to* SIMON, *as he helps* CHRISTINA *with the struggling* JACKIE). You
all right, Mostyn?
SIMON (*his face twisted as though with pain*). Yes, I'm all right. Just
bleeding a bit and I can't move my leg.
CHRISTINA (*to* JACKIE). Come, dear.

(SMITH *and* CHRISTINA, *one on either side, help* JACKIE, *still struggling and crying hysterically, out* L. *Progress is slow as she resists.*)

SMITH (*off* L). Quiet, Jackie, quiet.

(SIMON *leans back in the chair, exhausted. The handkerchief held against his knee is now bright red. The tom-toms and singing continue loudly through the interval.*)

CURTAIN.

ACT II.

SCENE 2.

SCENE.—*The same. Five minutes later.*

SIMON *is lying back in his chair exactly as when curtain fell on Scene* 1. *The handkerchief is still clasped to his knee. The window down* L *is now open, not shut. The pistol is no longer on the floor near* R. *In the* R *doorway* LOUISE *is standing, half concealed, watching* SIMON. *There is something furtive about her. The voices of* DR. BESSNER *and* SMITH *are heard off* L *as they approach.* LOUISE *exits* R.

DR. BESSNER (*entering* L). Where is he, then ? (*He sees* SIMON *and hurries to* L *of him.*) Ach !

(LOUISE *enters* R. SMITH *enters and moves* LC.)

LOUISE (*running forward to* R *of the* C *table*). Mon Dieu, what is it ? What has happened ?

SIMON. Damn !

LOUISE. I heard a shot. I run here as fast as I can—

(DR. BESSNER *kneels down by* SIMON *and opens his case. He examines* SIMON'S *leg and applies an emergency dressing during the following.*)

SMITH (*to* LOUISE). Now keep calm. There's just been a little accident . . .

LOUISE. An accident ? To Monsieur ?

SIMON (*faintly wincing as* BESSNER *handles him*). I don't want a fuss Louise, understand. Ouch !

DR. BESSNER. Nasty . . . very nasty . . .

(SMITH *crosses above the table to* LOUISE.)

LOUISE. Shall I fetch Madame ?

SIMON (*emphatically*). No !

SMITH (*taking* LOUISE *familiarly by the arm*). Now look here, my dear girl. There's absolutely no cause to get upset. See ? You've got to be sensible. I'm sure you're a very sensible girl.

LOUISE (*smiling coquettishly at him*). Oh, Monsieur ! I was so afraid ! I thought perhaps it is a rising of the Arabs ! They come to murder us all. My heart it was in my mouth !

SMITH (*patting her on the shoulder*). There, there ! It's all quite simple. We were just—er—playing about with a pistol, not realising it was loaded. Stupid of us, but there it is.

LOUISE. Oh, but they are so dangerous—pistols.

SMITH. They certainly are.

DR. BESSNER. Yes, it is a nasty wound. The bone is injured, and there has been loss of blood. It will be best, I think, if Mr. Mostyn is moved into my cabin. There is a second berth there, and I can look after him. The wound must be properly dressed. (*To* SMITH.) You will have to get for me boiling water so that I can sterilise my instruments. (*He finds the bullet in the chair.*) Ach, fortunately we shall not have to extract the bullet.

SIMON. Sounds most alarming ! Like a major operation !

DR. BESSNER. Not so. Much cannot be done here. I have not the means. (*He rises.*) I can but patch, you understand ? It is to hospital you must go. But have no fear. For two, three weeks you lie still and after that you walk as well as ever. (*He pats* SIMON *reassuringly on the shoulder; then crosses above him and puts his bag on the* C *table.*)

SIMON. Nice way of spending your honeymoon ! Thank goodness Kay hasn't woken up. She needn't know anything about it till the morning.

DR. BESSNER. I did not hear the shot myself—or rather, there are so many shots on the shore—and the jackals and the drums. Ah, but it is noisy here in the desert.

LOUISE. Can I get Monsieur his things from his cabin ?

SIMON. Yes, do. Pyjamas and my washing things. Be careful not to wake up Madame next door.

LOUISE. I understand. I will be very quiet, Monsieur.

(*She exits* R.)

SIMON. How's Jackie ?

DR. BESSNER. I have given her a sedative injection—a strong one. Already she has calmed down. In half an hour she will sleep.

SIMON. Good. She didn't really know what she was doing, poor kid. She was sozzled.

SMITH. We can fix up some story or other. Pity that French girl heard the row. However, I daresay we can manage to shut her mouth. But you can see already that she smells a rat.

SIMON. Get hold of that pistol before we forget it, will you, Smith ? It's over there somewhere—just about where you are.

SMITH (*searching* RC *to* R). I can't see any signs of it.

SIMON. It must be there. Perhaps it's rolled under something.

(SMITH *stoops and looks.*)

SMITH. There's no pistol here.

SIMON. But there must be. I saw her drop it. I heard it fall.

SMITH. Well, it's not here now. Perhaps Christina picked it up.

SIMON. I don't think she did . . . (*He thinks.*) I'm almost sure she didn't . . . She was hanging on to Jackie.

SMITH. Well, somebody must have picked it up. Perhaps Jackie herself did.

SIMON. No, she didn't.

(*The sound of the tom-toms and singing finally dies away.*)

DR. BESSNER (*crossing to* L *of* SIMON *and taking his arm*). Now, Mr. Mostyn, we get you to my cabin. Mr. Smith, you go that side.

(SMITH *crosses below the table to* SIMON'S R.)

Your arm under so—Right. Now lift. Your arms over our shoulders, Mr. Mostyn. I—

(*Together they raise* SIMON *to his feet.* LOUISE *screams off* R. *She enters* R, *screaming.*)

LOUISE. Oh my God ! Madame . . . Madame . . .

SMITH. Be quiet. Don't make that noise.

LOUISE. But Madame—Madame—she is *dead*—dead there in her bed !

SIMON (*with a great roar*). What's that ?

LOUISE. She has been shot—shot through the head.

(SIMON *makes a spring forward, tries to run, and collapses.*)

DR. BESSNER (*to* SIMON). Are you mad ? You cannot possibly walk, do you not understand ? (*He seats* SIMON *in the chair again and stands behind him.*)

(SMITH *crosses below the table to* LOUISE *at* RC.)

SIMON. But Kay—Kay—

SMITH (*shaking* LOUISE). Tell us. Tell us.

LOUISE. I went into Monsieur's cabin to get his pyjamas. The door into Madame's cabin was ajar, so I move very quietly not to wake here. Then I smell something . . . (*She sniffs.*) It is the same smell as in here. The smell there is when a gun is fired.

DR. BESSNER. Yes, yes ?

LOUISE. And it comes from Madame's cabin. So I go in. I go across to her bed. She lies there on her side. I think it is all right, but I listen and there is no breathing, you understand. So I switch on the light, and I see—I see Madame has been shot through the head. There is a little round hole here. (*She indicates her temple. She sits at the table down* R.)

(CANON PENNEFATHER *enters* L. *He is still fully dressed. He is followed by the* STEWARD.)

CANON (*coming* LC). What is this ? What has happened ? Who screamed ?

SMITH. Mrs. Mostyn has been shot.

CANON. Shot !

(*The* STEWARD *runs out* L.)

SIMON. Jackie has killed Kay . . .

DR. BESSNER. We must go and see. (*To* CANON PENNEFATHER.) You will come ?

CANON. At once !

(DR. BESSNER *and* CANON PENNEFATHER *go out* R. SIMON *buries his face in his hands.*)

SIMON. Kay . . . Kay . . .

(MCNAUGHT, *the ship's manager, enters* L *with the* STEWARD.)

MCNAUGHT. What's this ? Someone's been shot ? (*He comes down* LC.)

SMITH. Mrs. Mostyn.

MCNAUGHT. Dead ?

SMITH. The doctor has gone to see.

McNaught. This is a verra bad business. It's a thing that has never happened before. I'm at a loss to know the correct procedure.

Smith (*coming* c *below the table*). Are you in charge?

McNaught. I am. But as I say, a thing like this has never occurred before. Mrs. Mostyn's a verra important person, which doesn't make it easier. (*He looks at* Simon, *then moves* c *nearer to* Smith.) Is it known who shot the lady?

Smith. I'm afraid so.

McNaught. I see. I was about to obsairve that no one from on shore could have come on board. There's a guard always stationed on the bank. (*He moves away to* l.)

Smith (*following to* lc). Do you expect trouble, then?

McNaught. Nothing, but possibly some petty pilfering. That's all —but it means that nobody could have come on board unobsairved.

(*Enter* Canon Pennefather *and* Dr. Bessner r, *their faces grave.*)

Simon. Well?

(Canon Pennefather *crosses above the table* c *and lays his hand on* Simon's *shoulder in sympathy.* Dr. Bessner *slowly shakes his head.*)

Canon. She was shot through the right temple.

Dr. Bessner (*moving to* r *of* Canon Pennefather). Not very long ago. Perhaps five minutes—perhaps twenty minutes—not more. The pistol was held close against her head. That is clearly seen by the scorching of the skin.

Canon (*quoting*). "I want to put my dear little pistol close against her head, and then just press the trigger—so."

Simon. Who said that?

Canon. I think you can guess. Jacqueline de Severac said it to me on the night we left Shellal.

(McNaught *and the* Steward *exit* l.)

Simon. Kay wanted to get off the boat. If I'd only agreed! If I'd done what she wanted! Instead, I persuaded her to face it out . . .

Canon. Don't harrow yourself by going over the past. You couldn't know what was going to happen.

Simon. I knew Jackie.

(Smith *drops down* l.)

Canon. You're quite sure that it *was* Jackie who shot her?

Simon (*surprised*). Of course. Who else could it be? You don't mean—it couldn't be *suicide?* Kay would never . . .

Canon. It was not suicide. Kay was shot with a small calibre pistol—and the pistol has been taken away.

Dr. Bessner. It was, I should say, the same pistol that fired this. (*He shows the bullet.*) This is the bullet that through Mr. Mostyn's leg passed and lodged in the chair.

Simon (*to* Smith). You were right. My eyes weren't working. Jackie must have picked up that pistol—or else I'm dreaming and she never dropped it.

CANON (*moving behind* SIMON *to his* L). You are very sure it was Jacqueline ?

SIMON. You said that before, sir. Is there a doubt ?

CANON. I would only remind you that you are condemning someone unheard. Jacqueline has not had a chance of refuting the accusation against her. Where is she ?

DR. BESSNER. Mr. Smith came to me. He told me that the girl had shot Mr. Mostyn through the leg and was now in hysterics. I went with him to her cabin where I found her with Miss Grant trying to calm her. I gave her a strong injection.

CANON. It would make her sleep ?

DR. BESSNER. Yes, but not at once. There would be an interval of, say, half an hour. She would become calm, and then get drowsy.

SIMON. And I suppose as soon as she was left alone, she ran round the stern of the boat and shot Kay . . . She's not really responsible, you know—she's been drinking all the evening. The poor kid was half crazy. It's my fault—the whole bloody business. I'm the one to blame !

(MISS FFOLIOT-FFOULKES *enters* R. *She is very dignified in a rather peculiar négligé.*)

MISS FFOLIOT-FFOULKES. Has anything happened ? (*She comes* RC.)

SIMON (*hysterical*). Has anything happened ? Has anything happened ? That's funny—that's damned funny . . .

DR. BESSNER (*moving to* SIMON'S R *elbow*). Quiet, Mr. Mostyn, quiet. (*He gives a sharp twist to his shoulder.*)

SIMON. Thanks, Bessner. Sorry.

BESSNER. All this for you is very bad. I will give you now an injection. (*He opens his bag.*)

SIMON. I won't have it. Do you think *I* want to sleep ?

MISS FFOLIOT-FFOULKES. What is it ?

CANON (*crossing below the table to* MISS FFOLIOT-FFOULKES). Mrs. Mostyn has been murdered—shot through the head.

MISS FFOLIOT-FFOULKES. Shot ? In her cabin ? But that is quite close to mine. *I* might have been murdered.

SMITH. A mistake was made.

MISS FFOLIOT-FFOULKES. I call it disgraceful—absolutely disgraceful ! Proper safeguards should be taken. Natives should not be allowed to creep aboard in the night.

SMITH. Nobody has come aboard, Miss ffoliot-ffoulkes.

MISS FFOLIOT-FFOULKES. Nobody ?

SMITH. Nobody.

MISS FFOLIOT-FFOULKES. But then—

CANON. Surely if your cabin is near that of Mrs. Mostyn you heard the shot ?

MISS FFOLIOT-FFOULKES. I did not hear anything.

CANON. I see.

MISS FFOLIOT-FFOULKES. Where is Christina ? (*She crosses* CANON PENNEFATHER *to the chair* R *of the* C *table.*) I should have said the least she could do was to come and look after me. I might have had a serious heart attack with the shock. I might have been murdered. Where *is* Christina ?

CANON.   Isn't she in her cabin ?

MISS FFOLIOT-FFOULKES.   No.

CANON (*to* DR. BESSNER).   Dr. Bessner, will you go to Miss de Severac's cabin and ask Miss de Severac to come here ?

DR. BESSNER.   Certainly.

(*He goes out* L.)

MISS FFOLIOT-FFOULKES.   I suppose my niece has been murdered and her body flung overboard.

CANON.   I think that there is probably a much less melodramatic explanation of her absence.

MISS FFOLIOT-FFOULKES.   Nothing can excuse her heartless conduct in not coming to look after me. (*She sits* R *of the* C *table.*)

CANON.   I think it possible that Christina does not yet know there has been a murder on board. (*To* LOUISE.) Where do you sleep ? (*He moves to her.*)

LOUISE (*starting*).   Pardon ?

CANON.   Je vous demande, mademoiselle, où est vôtre cabine ?

LOUISE.   My cabin, Monsieur—it is next to that of Madame Mostyn. Beyond, you comprehend.

CANON.   Next door. And you did not hear the shot ?

LOUISE.   Oh, yes, Monsieur. I heard the shot. But I wake up and do not know what it is I hear. So I come along the deck and I find here Monsieur shot through the leg—so naturally, Monsieur, I think it is *that* shot I hear.

CANON.   And you heard no one on the deck outside your cabin ?

LOUISE.   No, no, I hear nothing.

CANON.   And you saw nothing ?

LOUISE (*with a trace of meaning*).   What should I see, Monsieur ?

CANON.   *I* am asking *you.*

MISS FFOLIOT-FFOULKES.   I heard footsteps running past my cabin—light, quick footsteps.

CANON.   But you said just now that you heard nothing at all.

MISS FFOLIOT-FFOULKES.   I know, but . . .

(SMITH *moves up* LC. DR. BESSNER *enters* L *with* JACKIE *and* CHRISTINA. JACKIE *is very pale and yawning incessantly. She seems half asleep. They put her in the chair down* L. CHRISTINA *stands on her* R. DR. BESSNER *stands behind her.*)

CHRISTINA.   Auntie . . .

MISS FFOLIOT-FFOULKES.   You wicked, heartless girl, where have you been ?

JACKIE.   What's happened ? (*In a dull voice, with frightful yawns.*) What's happened now ?

CHRISTINA.   I'm sorry, Aunt Helen ; I had to stay with Miss de Severac. She wasn't well, and I didn't like to leave her.

SMITH. How long have you been with her?

CHRISTINA (*slightly astonished*). I've not left her at all. Not since you and I got her to her cabin. I stayed with her, as you know, while you got Dr. Bessner and then after he gave her the injection she didn't seem to want to be left alone, so I stayed there.

SIMON (*transformed*). Is that true? My God, is that true?

(SMITH *sits against the table up* L.)

CHRISTINA. I'm not in the habit of telling lies, Mr. Mostyn. I don't know what you mean.

SIMON. Don't be offended, Christina. You don't understand, this is frightfully important. When Kay went to bed, Jackie was here, in the saloon, wasn't she?

CHRISTINA. Yes.

SIMON. And she never left until she went out with you?

(CHRISTINA *nods*.)

And since then you've not left her—not for a minute, is that right?

CHRISTINA. That's right.

SIMON. Thank God!

JACKIE. What's the matter? What are you talking about?

CANON (*coming down* RC). Kay has been shot . . .

JACKIE (*repeating it dully*). Kay has been shot . . . You mean she's dead? (*She takes it in slowly*.) . . . I see . . . you thought I'd shot her . . . But I didn't . . . I didn't . . .

CANON. We know that you didn't.

JACKIE. I can't seem to take it in . . . my head . . . I'm so terribly sleepy . . . Simon! Simon! I didn't kill Kay!

SIMON. It's all right, Jackie dear. It's all right.

JACKIE. It's *you* I shot.

SIMON. That doesn't matter. Listen, Jackie, keep awake a minute. Try to think. What did you do with the pistol after you shot me?

JACKIE. I dropped it—over there. (*She nods and indicates stage* R.)

(*They all look at each other.*)

DR. BESSNER (*to* CHRISTINA). Take her back and get her into bed. She is nearly unconscious now.

CHRISTINA (*raising* JACKIE). Come along, dear.

(CHRISTINA *and* JACKIE *go out* L. DR. BESSNER *moves to* SIMON.)

DR. BESSNER. Now, Mr. Mostyn, I insist that you let me give you a hypodermic. You are in pain, and you have now some fever. Mr. Smith and I will get you into my cabin, and I must then dress your knee properly.

SIMON. No—I tell you—no. Don't you understand? My wife has been murdered. *Murdered!* We've got to find out who killed her. Somebody on this boat killed her. It's incredible, fantastic, but it's true. Somebody who overheard the scene between me and Jackie here to-night, and who thought that Kay's death would be fixed on poor wretched little Jackie. That's right—(*appealing to* CANON PENNE-FATHER)—isn't it, sir? That's right?

CANON (*moving above the* C *table*). Yes. A new and very serious problem has arisen. But you are in pain, Simon, and you must have proper care and attention.

SIMON. I don't want care and attention. I want to find out who killed Kay.

(MCNAUGHT *enters* L *with the* STEWARD.)

CANON. It is a matter for the police.

MCNAUGHT. That's right, sir. I have just sent a fast launch that was here to Wadi Halfa. The police will arrive and take charge to-morrow morning. In the meantime we'll stay put, and I should be obliged if you yourself would take charge until then, sir, and make any interrogations you think fit. I'd be out of my depth.

CANON. I think that seems a very sensible suggestion.

MCNAUGHT. Very good, sir. Then I'll leave you now. I'll interview the crew and the stewards right away and find out if they know anything or have seen anything. I don't know if any of you gentlemen know Arabic ? (*Heads are shaken.*) Right, then you'd best leave that part of it to me. See you later, gentlemen !

(*He goes out* L. *He says something to the* STEWARD *in Arabic. The* STEWARD *follows him.*)

MISS FFOLIOT-FFOULKES. This is all very distressing, dear Canon.

CANON (*coldly*). As you say, very distressing. (*He turns up* R.)

MISS FFOLIOT-FFOULKES. I think, as there is nothing *I* can do, I will go back to my cabin and try to sleep. (*She rises.*) Please send Christina to me. I cannot imagine why she seems to feel an obligation to look after someone who is, after all, a *mere* acquaintance. (*She moves towards the door* R.)

CANON (*coming down* L *of her*). Just a minute, Miss ffoliot-ffoulkes. Anything that anyone saw or heard this evening is of importance. You say you heard footsteps running along the deck. Have you any idea what time that was ?

MISS FFOLIOT-FFOULKES. I really could not say.

CANON. In which direction were they going, fore or aft ?

MISS FFOLIOT-FFOULKES. I really couldn't tell you. (*She looks at him very blankly.*)

CANON. Thank you very much. Good night.

(MISS FFOLIOT-FFOULKES *goes out* R *quickly.*)

DR. BESSNER (*about to sit at the table down* L). Ach, what a draught there is. It is cold at nights in the desert. (*He shuts the window and sits.*)

SIMON. Could that old woman have killed Kay ? No, impossible ! Why should she ?

CANON (*shaking his head*). It would be as well, I think, for each one of us to state briefly exactly what he did this evening after Mrs. Mostyn left us to go to her cabin.

SIMON. I was in here. Bessner went to bed soon after you did ; Smith after that.

CANON. Dr. Bessner ?
BESSNER. I went straight to my cabin. I undressed. I was in my bunk when Mr. Smith came to rouse me and told me that Mr: Mostyn had been shot and that Miss de Severac was in hysterics.
CANON. You did not leave your cabin ?
DR. BESSNER. No.
CANON. You did nòt go round to the port side of the deck ?
DR. BESSNER. Certainly not.
CANON. Thank you. Mr. Smith ?
SMITH. Quite the examining magistrate, aren't you ?
CANON. I have, unfortunately, not the powers of one.
SMITH (*putting one foot on the chair above the table*). Well, conceding you for the moment the divine right to ask questions, I left the saloon about five minutes before Jackie started her shooting stunt. She was working up for it nicely with dollops of brandy and a bit of crooning. It got embarrassing and I cleared out—by that door. (*He points* L.) I did not spring round the deck and shoot Kay Mostyn for the excellent reason that Jackie had tight hold of the pistol. I strolled along the deck and listened to the howling of the jackals and the singing of some Bedouin —I don't know which made the worst noise. Then I heard a commotion in here and Christina giving a nice sensible controlled Scottish version of a scream, and I came hurrying in. After that I have an alibi, being in the company of Christina, Jackie, and Dr. Bessner.
CANON. Thank you, Mr. Smith.
SMITH. I have no divine right, but may I ask you the same question ? Where were you, Canon Pennefather, after you left the saloon ?
CANON. I went to my cabin.
SMITH. Just like Dr. Bessner ?
CANON. Yes.
SMITH. But you didn't go to bed ?
CANON. No. I was reading. (*To* SIMON.) Where exactly did Jacqueline drop the pistol after shooting you ?
SIMON (*pointing to* R). In that doorway.

(CANON PENNEFATHER *goes over there.*)

There, just where you are now.

(CANON PENNEFATHER *looks down at the doorway, then through it on to the deck.*)

CANON (*moving to the chair* R *of the* C *table*). You were in a good deal of pain, Simon ? (*He sits.*)
SIMON. Yes.
CANON. Did you close your eyes, or did you keep them open ?
SIMON. I felt a bit sick—faint. I leaned back and shut my eyes. It's rather idiotic, but the sight of blood makes me feel queer.
CANON. Quite so. Therefore, during those few minutes when you were alone, someone might have crept up to this doorway and picked up the pistol without your seeing or hearing them ?
SIMON. Oh yes, easily.

CANON. Someone who may have been on the deck outside and who had overheard all that had led up to the final outburst. (*His eyes come slowly round to* LOUISE.)

LOUISE. Monsieur?

CANON. Come here, Louise.

(LOUISE *rises and comes forward slowly*.)

Have you been telling us the truth, my girl?

LOUISE. O Monsieur, how can you doubt?

CANON. I do doubt. What do you know about this crime?

LOUISE. Nothing, Monsieur—nothing at all. Ah, you accuse me? Me, a respectable girl! I swear to you—

CANON. Pas tant d'histoires, Louise. Il faut dire la vérité.

LOUISE. Ah, Monsieur l'Abbé, ne vous doutez pas de moi! Cette pauvre Madame Mostyn, elle avait tant d'esprit, tant de beauté—tout le mond l'aimait. Qui donc aurait pu tuer une femme comme ça, jeune et belle?

(CANON PENNEFATHER *watches her.*)

CANON (*rising*). Allons, pas des blagues!

(LOUISE *stops dead.*)

What did you see or hear to-night?

LOUISE (*making her words very significant*). But what should I see? Naturally, if I had looked out in time, I should have seen this monster, this assassin, whoever he is, leave Madame's cabin . . . I should know then who he was. But what can I say? What can I do?

SIMON. My good girl, don't be a fool. Nobody thinks you saw or heard anything if you say you didn't. Nobody's accusing you of anything. You'll be all right. *I'll* look after you.

LOUISE. Monsieur is too kind!

SIMON. Just tell us exactly what you did to-night. That's all Canon Pennefather wants to know.

LOUISE. Madame had told me I could go to bed. She would not want me, as she might be sitting up late. So I went to my cabin about ten. I made myself my tea of camomille, as usual. But somehow it tasted bitter, not good . . . the heat, perhaps . . . so I threw it away. (*She pauses.*) After that I went to bed, but I did not sleep. It was too hot and the little flies of the sand, they stung me. I put some Flit about and again I try to go to sleep.

CANON. And after that?

LOUISE. After that—nothing. There is much noise—ces sales Arabes, they do not seem to sleep. Ah, it is without doubt one of them, un de ces types—who crept on board and killed Madame. They have the hot blood! They hate, perhaps, these fair Englishwomen who are so arrogant . . .

CANON. Did *you* hate your mistress, Louise?

LOUISE. I, Monsieur? I was devoted to Madame!

CANON. I wonder.

LOUISE (*crossing down stage to* SIMON). Monsieur, you will protect me. The uncle of Madame, he is trying to say that I killed her.

CANON. Perhaps you did.

LOUISE (*shrilly*). Ah, it is an outrage! C'est infâme!

SIMON. Oh, calm down, Louise! Go off and go to bed. We'll talk to you in the morning.

LOUISE. Very well, Monsieur. Good night, Monsieur. (*As she moves to* CANON PENNEFATHER.) Good night. It was a joke, was it not, what you said? Some jokes are very funny. That one was not.

CANON. Some jokes are dangerous.

LOUISE. Yes, they are dangerous.

(*She crosses to the door* R *and exits.* SIMON *gives a groan and collapses.*)

DR. BESSNER (*rising*). Ach, what did I tell you? It is the shock. (*He hurries to* SIMON. *To* SMITH.) Help me. We must get him to my cabin.

SMITH (*moving to the door* L *and calling*). Hi, boy!

(*The* STEWARD *runs in* L.)

(*To* DR. BESSNER.) He'll help you. I want to speak to Canon Pennefather.

(DR. BESSNER *and the* STEWARD *carry* SIMON *out* L. *There is a pause.* CANON PENNEFATHER *and* SMITH *look at each other.* SMITH *moves in to* L *of the* C *table.*)

CANON. Well, Mr. Smith?

SMITH. Hope he's all right. (*Deliberately, with significance.*) It wouldn't suit your books if he pegged out, would it?

CANON. What do you mean, young man?

SMITH. I mean that whereas Mrs. Mostyn read through all documents before signing them, Simon Mostyn is a trusting fellow who will be content to sign on the dotted line.

CANON. I don't think I understand you, Mr. Smith.

SMITH. No? You think that because I play the fool I can't be serious. I'm serious now. Murder doesn't amuse me.

CANON. I'm glad to hear it.

SMITH. I've been wrong about you. I thought you were just the usual sort of canting society hypocrite, but you're something more : you're a fanatic. You believe in your new Jerusalem. A new Jerusalem needs money—and you've had money passing through your hands— Kay Ridgeway's money.

CANON (*smiling*). Oh, really, Mr. Smith, this is childish!

SMITH. Remember, I saw you in the King David Hotel in Jerusalem reading a great wad of mail? I suggest that you knew all about Kay's marriage, and that your surprise at meeting her here was just an act.

CANON. You are really a most intelligent young man, Mr. Smith. You're quite right.

SMITH (*slightly disconcerted*). Oh, so you admit that ?
CANON. I admit that.
SMITH. Well then ?
CANON. Well then, Mr. Smith ?

CURTAIN.

ACT III.

SCENE.—*The same. The following morning. The Temple of Abu Simbel is now visible through the windows.*

CANON PENNEFATHER *is in the chair below the table up* L. *There is a bundle on a tray on the table in front of him.* DR. BESSNER *enters* L.

CANON. How is your patient this morning, doctor?

DR. BESSNER (*crossing to the window up* C). I have done what can be done—but he should be got to hospital as soon as possible. I hope the police will soon arrive. I would like an X-ray. There is much inflammation and a rise of temperature. He asks questions and refuses any further sedatives.

CANON. That is perhaps natural. The shock of his wife's death must have been very great.

DR. BESSNER. What have you there? (*He moves to the table.*)

CANON. These were fished in a bundle out of the river by two of the boatmen. It had obviously been thrown from this boat and had stuck in the mud.

DR. BESSNER (*fingering the bundle*). Ah, a piece of velvet—a velvet scarf—and a handkerchief—a bottle—and—aha! a pistol. Is it the right pistol?

CANON. It is the pistol with which Jacqueline shot Simon Mostyn last night—(*pointing to the initials*) J.S. (*He hands the pistol to* DR. BESSNER.)

DR. BESSNER. And it is also the pistol with which Mrs. Mostyn was shot.

CANON. You are sure of that?

DR. BESSNER. No, one cannot be sure—that is a police matter—it is for the expert in—ballistics, I think you call it. Only they can say with certainty that a bullet has been fired from a particular weapon. It is the right calibre. (*He breaks the pistol.*) And two shots, I see, have been fired.

CANON. Yes, there seems very little doubt about it.

DR. BESSNER. But perhaps I should not be handling it?

CANON. There can be no fingerprints. It is soaked in river mud.

DR. BESSNER (*nodding, putting down the pistol and picking up the scarf*). Ah, this is interesting! (*He holds it up.*) See the bullet holes. This was wrapped round the pistol, so! (*He demonstrates.*) And the pistol fired through the material. That, I suppose, in order to deaden the noise of the report.

(CHRISTINA *enters* R.)

CHRISTINA (*crossing to* DR. BESSNER). Why, that's Aunt Helen's scarf—the one she couldn't find last night! She's been so annoyed with me about it—says I ought to have looked after it.

DR. BESSNER. Ach, but it is not your fault. Always I have observed most conscientious you are. (*He beams and pats her on the shoulder. He hands the scarf to* CANON PENNEFATHER.)

(SMITH *enters* L.)

SMITH. Doctor, Mostyn wants you. He's all het up—insists on being got up and brought here.

DR. BESSNER. That I have expressly forbidden! Already he has fever. He must remain quiet. Ah, these healthy young men—they are the most difficult patients when they are ill. I must be stern—very stern.

(*He exits* L, *hurriedly.* CANON PENNEFATHER *rises and moves to the window up* RC. *He holds the scarf in his hands and frowns. He pays no attention to the scene between* SMITH *and* CHRISTINA.)

SMITH (*moving down* C). That stout medico seems to have fallen for you, Christina. Take my advice and have nothing to do with him. He's a dirty old man.

CHRISTINA (*coming down* L *of the* C *table to* SMITH). Dr. Bessner is a very clever man. He knows a lot. He's a psychologist.

SMITH. I've never heard it called that before!

CHRISTINA. I don't know what you mean. Anyway, he's a very learned man and he's *kind*.

SMITH. What a girl! She likes everyone! Christina Grant, you're the only really nice woman I've ever come across. Will you marry me?

CHRISTINA (*equably*). Don't be so foolish.

SMITH. That's not the way to reply to a genuine offer of marriage—made before a witness, too. I've deliberately offered you marriage against all my principles, because I don't believe you'd stand for anything else, so marriage it shall be. Come on, Christina, say yes.

CHRISTINA. You ought to be ashamed of your foolishness. The trouble with you is that you're not serious.

SMITH. Not serious over my offer? I am.

CHRISTINA. I meant your character. You laugh at things you shouldn't laugh at. I doubt very much whether you'll make a reliable husband.

SMITH. But Christina, you'd easily be reliable enough for two!

CHRISTINA. That's enough.

(MISS FFOLIOT-FFOULKES *enters* R. SMITH *moves up* R.)

MISS FFOLIOT-FFOULKES. So there you are, Christina—as usual, when I want you. (*She crosses to* R *of the table* C.)

CANON (*coming down* RC). Good morning, Miss ffoliot-ffoulkes, I think this is the scarf you were looking for last night?

(CHRISTINA *goes out* L.)

MISS FFOLIOT-FFOULKES. The one Christina mislaid so carelessly. Just look at the state it's in. Disgraceful! It's all wet—and covered with mud. What has someone been doing with it?

CANON. Someone has used it—for murder.

MISS FFOLIOT-FFOULKES. My scarf! What impertinence!

CANON. Quite. When is the last time you remember having it?

MISS FFOLIOT-FFOULKES. I had it in here before I went in to dinner last night. Christina should not have let me leave it behind.

CANON. This is not your handkerchief, Miss ffoliot-ffoulkes?

MISS FFOLIOT-FFOULKES (*with disgust*). No, indeed. It's a man's and a nasty cotton thing.

CANON. It's just an ordinary Woolworth's handkerchief—stained pink. No mark on it, not even a laundry mark.

MISS FFOLIOT-FFOULKES. I suppose I can take my property—even though it *has* been completely ruined. I shall sue the company.

CANON. These things will have to be shown first to the police.

MISS FFOLIOT-FFOULKES (*sharply*). The police.

CANON. A police launch is on its way. It may arrive at any minute.

MISS FFOLIOT-FFOULKES (*sitting R of the C table*). Oh, I see.

(CANON PENNEFATHER *moves up* C *to the window, frowning over the scarf and handkerchief.*)

SMITH (*coming down* RC *and crossing to* C *below the table*). I've been hoping to get you alone, Miss ffoliot-ffoulkes.

MISS FFOLIOT-FFOULKES. Indeed, Mr.—er—Smith, I can't imagine for what reason.

SMITH. Just this. I want to marry your niece.

MISS FFOLIOT-FFOULKES. You must be out of your senses, young man.

SMITH. Not at all. I'm determined to marry her. I've asked her to marry me

MISS FFOLIOT-FFOULKES. Indeed? And I presume she sent you about your business?

SMITH. She refused me.

MISS FFOLIOT-FFOULKES (*sitting back*). Naturally.

SMITH. Not naturally at all. I'm going to go on asking her till she agrees.

MISS FFOLIOT-FFOULKES. I can assure you, Mr. Smith, that I shall take steps to see that my niece is not subject to any such persecution.

SMITH. Come now, what have you got against me?

MISS FFOLIOT-FFOULKES. I should think that was quite obvious, Mr.—er—

SMITH. Smith is the name—one of the Hammer Smiths!

MISS FFOLIOT-FFOULKES. Mr. Smith. Any such idea is quite out of the question.

SMITH. You mean that I'm not good enough for her?

MISS FFOLIOT-FFOULKES. I should have thought that would have been obvious to you.

SMITH. In what way am I not good enough? (MISS FFOLIOT-FFOULKES *does not answer*.) Come now. I've got two legs, two arms, good health and quite reasonable brains. What's wrong with that?

MISS FFOLIOT-FFOULKES. There is such a thing as social position.

SMITH. Social position is bunk.

(CHRISTINA *enters* L.)

(*Turning.*) Come along Christina. I'm asking for your hand in marriage in the best conventional manner.

MISS FFOLIOT-FFOULKES. Christina, have you encouraged this young man?

CHRISTINA (*coming down* LC). I—no—of course not—at least—not exactly—I mean—

MISS FFOLIOT-FFOULKES. What do you mean?

SMITH. She hasn't encouraged me. I've done it all. She hasn't actually pushed me in the face because she's got too kind a heart. Christina, your aunt says I'm not good enough for you. That, of course, is true, but not in the way she means it. My moral nature certainly doesn't equal yours, but her point is that I am hopelessly below you socially.

MISS FFOLIOT-FFOULKES. That, I think, is equally obvious to Christina.

SMITH. Is it? (*He looks at* CHRISTINA *searchingly*.) Is that why you won't marry me?

CHRISTINA. No, it isn't. If—if I liked you, I'd marry you, no matter what you were.

SMITH. But you don't like me?

CHRISTINA. I—I think you're just outrageous. The way you say things—the things you say! I—I've never met anyone the least like you. I . . .

(*She crosses and rushes out* R.)

SMITH (*sitting left of the table* C). On the whole, that's not too bad a start. (*He leans back and whistles*.) I'll be calling you Auntie yet.

MISS FFOLIOT-FFOULKES. Canon Pennefather, will you make this young man leave the room at once? (*To* SMITH.) If you don't leave here at once, sir, I'll ring for the steward and get you put out.

SMITH. I've paid for my ticket. You can't possibly turn me out of the public saloon. (*He rises*.) But I'll humour you— (*He goes to the door* L.) Auntie!

(*He goes out* L.)

MISS FFOLIOT-FFOULKES. Oh dear! I feel most upset! That dreadful insolent young man!

CANON (*crossing down* R). Rather eccentric, perhaps. Most of that family are. Always inclined to tilt at windmills. That's why he won't use his title, of course.

MISS FFOLIOT-FFOULKES (*sharply*). Title?

CANON. Oh yes, didn't you recognise him? He's young Lord Dawlish. As I say, all the Hargrave-Smythes are eccentric. He drops his title and calls himself plain Smith. I believe he is a member of the Communist Party. But actually rolling in money, of course.

MISS FFOLIOT-FFOULKES. Indeed? . . . Indeed? Most interesting. (*She rises*.) I am much obliged to you for telling me this, dear Canon Pennefather. I think perhaps I had better have a word with Christina.

(*She goes out* R. SIMON, *supported by* DR. BESSNER *and the* STEWARD, *enters* L. SIMON *looks ill and feverish*. SMITH *re-enters with them. They bring* SIMON *to the chair* L *of the* C *table*. DR. BESSNER *is above* SIMON *at his* R. *He carries his bag*.)

CANON. Ah, Simon. Feeling better this morning ?

SIMON. Oh, I'm all right.

(*The* STEWARD *moves to the door* L *and waits.* SMITH *stands* LC.)

DR. BESSNER (*angrily*). Madness, I tell you, madness ! Do you wish to kill yourself, Mr. Mostyn ? I tell you all this excitement—all this movement, it is most injurious. Let me at least give you an injection. (*He opens his bag.*)

SIMON (*waving him aside*). Don't you see that I can't stay quietly in your cabin being treated like an invalid ? Don't you realise that my wife was shot last night ? What the hell does it matter what happens to me ? Not that anything will. I'm as strong as a horse. But I've got to be in the centre of things, to know what is going on. I've got to find out . . . (*He stops in sudden faintness.*)

DR. BESSNER. You see— (*He approaches* SIMON *with the hypodermic.*)

SIMON. Take that dope away. A drop of brandy is what I want.

DR. BESSNER. Brandy will be very injurious to your wound.

SIMON. Boy ! (*To the* STEWARD.) Double brandy, boy.

(*The* STEWARD *exits* L.)

DR. BESSNER. You are impossible. I wash my hands.

(*He goes out* L, *angrily.*)

SIMON. I'm sorry, but I can't stand being treated as a patient to be humoured and doctored and shut away from things. I want to know what's happening. Jackie didn't kill Kay. So who did ? Are we any nearer ?

SMITH (*looking towards* CANON PENNEFATHER). Yes, I think we are.

SIMON. Have you seen Jackie this morning ?

SMITH. No, she's in her cabin.

SIMON. I must see her. I simply must see her. Smith, ask her to come here, will you ? There's a good chap.

(SMITH *nods and goes out* L.)

CANON (*moving up* RC). These things were fished out of the river in a bundle this morning. A scarf, a handkerchief, a bottle labelled "Nail Varnish" and this— (*He shows the pistol.*)

SIMON. Jackie's pistol ?

CANON (*coming above the* C *table*). Yes, with two shots fired.

SIMON. So someone did creep along to that door last night and pick it up. Someone who meant Jackie to take the rap. That's what makes my blood boil. Framing poor little Jackie. Jackie, who wouldn't hurt a fly !

CANON (*looking at* SIMON'S *leg*). My dear Simon !

SIMON. Oh, *that* ! That's different. I more or less asked for that.

(*The* STEWARD *enters with a drink, hands it to* SIMON *and exits.*)

CANON (*sitting above the table*). Who do you think shot Kay ? Louise ?

SIMON (*slowly*). Somehow, I don't think it was Louise.

CANON. Her manner last night was odd, to say the least of it.

SIMON. Yes, she knows something.   I grant you that.   And I believe
I can get out of her what she knows.

(JACKIE *runs in* L.   *She looks pale and upset.*)

Jackie dear !

JACKIE (*suddenly running and kneeling down by* SIMON).   Oh, Simon,
Simon, can you ever forgive me ?   I must have been mad—quite mad !
(*She sobs.*)

SIMON (*awkwardly*).   Not mad—just a bit tight, that's all.

JACKIE (*sobbing*).   I might have killed you.

SIMON (*cheerfully*).   Not with a rotten little pea-shooter like that.

JACKIE.   And your leg—perhaps you'll never walk again !

SIMON.   Now look here, Jackie, don't be maudlin.   As soon as we get
to Assouan they're going to put the X-rays to work and see just what the
damage is, and fix me up in no time.   So, don't get all het up.   I thought
you might be worrying a bit.

JACKIE (*half laughing, half crying*).   Worrying a bit ?   Oh, Simon !

SIMON.   That's all right.   You've always been a bit hot-tempered.

JACKIE.   I'm a devil—that's what I am—a devil.   But I didn't kill
Kay—you *do* know that, don't you ?

SIMON.   Everybody knows that, thank goodness.   Listen, Jackie, I
think we've got a chance of getting at the truth of the matter through
Louise.

JACKIE (*startled*).   Through Louise ?

SIMON.   Yes.   The Canon and I both thought her manner peculiar
last night.   We think she knows something.

JACKIE.   What could she know ?

SIMON (*slowly*).   There's a chance, I suppose, that she looked out of
her cabin last night—and saw something—(*pause*) something or someone.

JACKIE.   But then—(*frown*) why doesn't she say so ?

SIMON.   Because in my opinion she's out for blackmail.   Do you
agree, sir ?

CANON.   I think there is every indication of it.

SIMON.   Now in my opinion there's only one way to make her speak—
bribery.   Bribery in a big way.

JACKIE.   Isn't that—I don't quite understand.

SIMON.   If Louise tells what she knows—that will send someone to the
scaffold.   (*He pauses.*)   Consequently she hopes to get large sums out of
that person.   You see ?

JACKIE.   Yes.   Horrible creature !

SIMON.   I've always thought she was a dangerous piece of goods.   But
that's not the point.   My idea is to bid higher than the other person.
I'll get her in here, tackle her, and offer her something so substantial
that she'll be willing to open her mouth as wide as we like.   (*With
emphasis.*)   That's our chance.   We mustn't miss it.

JACKIE.   Must it be—that way ?   I don't like it.

SIMON.   It's got to be settled quickly.   It's got to be *done now*.   (*He
looks very hard at her.   To* CANON PENNEFATHER.)   You agree, sir ?

CANON (*rising and moving away up* R).   No.   I am opposed to this idea of bribing a witness.   I agree with Jacqueline.   I don't like it.

SIMON.   But if we get results ?

CANON.   No.   The whole principle is wrong.

SIMON.   I tell you nothing but money will unloosen that girl's tongue.

(JACKIE *rises*.)

CANON.   How do you know that she will tell you the truth ?

SIMON.   She'll tell the truth if we make it worth her while.

JACKIE (*crossing slowly to* C).   Tell me, was Kay really shot with my pistol ?   Do you know for certain ?

CANON.   The bullet was of the same calibre.   We can only know for sure after the police have examined it.

JACKIE.   Somebody else on board might have had a pistol.

SIMON.   Bessner has a revolver.   But of course that's a thirty-five.

CANON.   I don't like this idea of yours, Simon.

(JACKIE *goes out* R.)

SIMON.   I'm sorry you don't agree, sir, but I'm going to try it all the same.

CANON.   I won't have any part in it.   (*He crosses up stage towards the door* L.)

SIMON.   Don't go away.   At least stand by and hear how it goes.

CANON.   No.   I won't co-operate in any way.

SIMON.   Well, send Bessner here.   There ought to be a witness. Otherwise she may deny the whole thing afterwards, no matter what she has said.   And tell Louise I want to see her.

CANON.   Very well.   Oh, here's Smith.   He'll do for you.

(CANON PENNEFATHER *goes out* L.)

CANON (*off; calling*).   Smith !

(SMITH *enters* L.)

SMITH.   What's the big idea ?

SIMON (*grinning*).   Bribery and corruption.

SMITH.   Oh, that's it, is it ?

SIMON.   The Canon objects—on principle.   I hope you don't.

SMITH.   I've no principles.

SIMON.   Good.   Now you efface yourself over there (*he indicates the table up* R) and just listen to all that goes on.

SMITH.   I become part of the background.   (*He crosses to the table up* R, *sits* R *of it, and picks up a magazine*.)

(LOUISE *enters* L.   *She looks wary and on her guard*.)

LOUISE (*coming* LC).   Monsieur wished to see me ?

SIMON.   Yes, I do.   Sit down, Louise.

(LOUISE *is about to sit down* L.)

No—there.   (*He indicates the chair* R *of the* C *table*.)

(LOUISE *crosses and sits, warily*.)

Have a cigarette ?   (*He extends his case to her*.)

LOUISE.   Oh no, Monsieur !

SIMON.   Come on.

LOUISE.   Monsieur is very kind.   (*She takes one.*)

SIMON.   I've always thought you were a smart girl, Louise.

LOUISE.   Thank you, Monsieur.

SIMON.   And that's why I want your help over this very sad business.

LOUISE (*sighing*).   It is indeed sad.   Madame was so young, so beautiful, so rich.

SIMON.   We've got to find out who did it, Louise.   That's very important.

LOUISE.   Of course, Monsieur.

SIMON.   So you will help, won't you ?

LOUISE.   Monsieur wishes my help—to find out who killed Madame ? (*There is slight mockery in her tone.*)

SIMON.   Yes, you're a very clever girl, Louise.

LOUISE.   You said so before, Monsieur.

SIMON.   Because it's true.   You're not very rich, are you, Louise ? Would you like to be rich ?

LOUISE (*with quick glance towards* SMITH *behind his paper*).   What a question, Monsieur !   Naturally the answer is yes.   But it is not likely. (*She sighs.*)

SIMON.   I think it's quite likely.

LOUISE.   I do not understand in the least what Monsieur means.

SIMON.   I'm offering you money, Louise—for the truth.

LOUISE (*in a peculiar tone*).   For the truth !

SIMON.   I think we understand each other.

LOUISE (*smiling, demurely*).   I do not understand at all.

SIMON.   Quite the wide-eyed innocent, aren't you, my girl ?   Now then, let's come down to brass tacks.   If you had looked out of your cabin at a certain moment last night—aroused, perhaps by a shot—not the shot that wounded me—(*he looks down at his leg*) but the shot that killed my wife—you might have seen—now, what might you have seen ?

LOUISE.   It is you who tell me !

SIMON.   I am suggesting that *you* should tell.

LOUISE.   Tell what I saw—that is, if I saw anything at all ?

SIMON.   Exactly.   You might have seen, perhaps, a person.

LOUISE.   I might have.   I do not say I did.

SIMON.   But I say you did.   You are keeping that knowledge to yourself—to sell it to someone who will buy it.   Sell it to me, Louise.

LOUISE (*uneasy*).   I do not understand you, Monsieur.

SIMON (*leaning forward*).   Sell it to me.

(*A revolver barrel shows through the deck window* R.)

How much do you want ?   A thousand pounds ?—two thousand— ?

(*The revolver fires.*   LOUISE *drops.*)

SMITH (*rising*).   My God !   (*He rushes forward to* LOUISE.)

SIMON (*trying to get up and falling back with a cry of pain*).   Damn this leg.   Is she badly hurt ?

SMITH. She's bleeding very badly. (*He crosses to the door* L.) Doctor ! Doctor Bessner !

(BESSNER *enters* L.)

DR. BESSNER. Was ist das ?

(SMITH *and* DR. BESSNER *cross to* LOUISE. JACKIE *enters* R.)

JACKIE (*entering*). Simon—Simon—are you all right ? Oh ! (*With relief.*) I thought you'd been shot. (*She crosses to him, to his* L.)

(SIMON *puts an arm round* JACKIE. DR. BESSNER *examines* LOUISE. CANON PENNEFATHER *comes in* L.)

CANON. What has happened ?

(MISS FFOLIOT-FFOULKES *enters* R *with* CHRISTINA.)

SMITH. She was shot through that window—

(*He rushes out* R, *colliding with* MISS FFOLIOT-FFOULKES *in the doorway. She turns her head to look after him malevolently.*)

DR. BESSNER. She is not quite dead—but she is dying.
CANON (*crossing above the table to* LOUISE). Will she speak ?
DR. BESSNER. Impossible. If you will help me, we will take her into her cabin and see what can be done—but I do not think anything will be any good.

(CANON PENNEFATHER *and* DR. BESSNER *take* LOUISE *out* R. SIMON *and* JACKIE *stare at* MISS FFOLIOT-FFOULKES *who seems quite unmoved.*)

MISS FFOLIOT-FFOULKES. All this is most disturbing. (*She comes to the table down* R *and sits.*) Christina, give me my knitting.

(CHRISTINA *hands her the knitting.*)

JACKIE (*crossing to down* C). Disturbing ! (*She begins to laugh hysterically.*) Two deaths—disturbing !
SIMON. Quiet, Jackie. Don't let go.
JACKIE. It's all so horrible.
SIMON. I know—I know. It's over now.

(JACKIE *turns and looks at him.*)

JACKIE. Simon—you're ill—you look very bad. (*She goes to him and takes his hands.*)
SIMON. All this excitement isn't the best thing for one. It's all right, Jackie, only a bit of fever.
JACKIE. Your hands are burning. Are you in pain ?
SIMON. It's my head going round. Light-headed. I mustn't be light-headed. Not now when it's all over. I've got to—I've got to—what have I got to do ?
JACKIE. You've got to find out who killed Kay.
SIMON. That's right. Hang on to that. Kay—Kay—who's Kay ? Of course—she's your best friend, isn't she, Jackie ?

(JACKIE *turns away up* LC *with a sob.* CANON PENNEFATHER *enters* R. *He is very grave.*)

JACKIE. How—how is she ?
CANON (*moving up* RC). Dead.
MISS FFOLIOT-FFOULKES. Oh, I should never have come on this cruise.
I came for rest and a change of air. (*She rises.*) Come, Christina. (*She
hands the knitting to* CHRISTINA.)

(DR. BESSNER *enters* R.   MISS FFOLIOT-FFOULKES *and* CHRISTINA *go
out* R.)

JACKIE (*coming above the table* C).   Doctor, Simon—he's ill—feverish.
DR. BESSNER (*crossing down stage to* SIMON).   Naturally he is ill.   It
is most dangerous what he insists on doing.   He should have remained
quietly in my cabin.   Now—(*feels pulse*) yes, now he has fever.   Come,
all this has been suicidal madness . . .
JACKIE.   Suicidal ?   He's not going to die ?
DR. BESSNER (*annoyed*).   Of course not, of course not, young lady !
I am vexed, that is all.   (*Calling.*) Boy !   (*To* SIMON.) Now I take
charge of you, young man, and I do not permit any more madnesses.
JACKIE.   Can I come with him ?

(*The* STEWARD *enters* L.)

DR. BESSNER.   No.   He needs quiet.
JACKIE.   But please . . .
DR. BESSNER.   He is my patient, and I cannot have him excited.

(JACKIE *makes a gesture of despair.*   SIMON *is carried out* L *between*
DR. BESSNER *and the* STEWARD.   JACKIE *follows.*   SMITH *enters* R.)

DR. BESSNER (*off*).   I shall give him an injection.
SMITH (*crossing to* L).   He's always wanting to give someone an
injection.   I shall suggest he gives one—lethal—to my aunt-to-be.
CANON.   I think you will find, Mr. Smith, that Miss ffoliot-ffoulkes has
undergone a change of heart.
SMITH.   What do you mean ?
CANON.   She knows that you wear your Smith with a hyphen.
SMITH (*turning*).   Who told her that ?
CANON.   I did.
SMITH.   Damned cheek . . .

(CHRISTINA *looks in* R, *sees* SMITH *and retreats.*)
Hi—Christina !

(*He hurries off* R.   CANON PENNEFATHER *sits down in the chair*
SIMON *sat in the previous night.   He holds the scarf in his hand, examines
it.   He thinks, shakes his head.   Then, rather obviously, an idea comes.
He looks at the window.   Slowly he wraps the pistol in the scarf and
holds it.   Leans back, closes eyes.   Then slowly nods his head.   He
brings out the small bottle.   Looks at it, unscrews the top—smells it—
puts a drop on the handkerchief—red ?   Shakes his head.   He puts it
down on the table.   Then he gets up and goes* R.   *Looks out along the
deck aft.   Then stands where* JACKIE *stood the night before, staring at*

SIMON'S *chair. He begins to hunt about. Finally, with an exclamation, he finds a bullet in the floor near* SIMON'S *chair. He digs it out with his penknife and stands holding it in his hand.* JACKIE *enters dejectedly* L.)

JACKIE. Simon's so ill . . . What's that you are holding ?
CANON. A bullet. (*He holds it out to her.*)
(JACKIE *is startled. She looks up from it to his face.*)
JACKIE. Where did you find it ?
CANON. Embedded in the floor there.
JACKIE. Is it—is it important ?
(CANON PENNEFATHER *slowly nods his head.*)
CANON. It means that I know now how Kay was killed.
JACKIE. I don't understand.
CANON. This scarf has been wrapped round a pistol and the pistol fired through it. This is evident by the scorching and the bullet holes. (*He shows her.* JACKIE *nods.*) It was suggested that this was done in order to muffle the sound of the shot that killed Kay. But Dr. Bessner stated quite clearly last night that the bullet hole in Kay's temple showed scorching, thereby proving that the pistol has been held close against her head. So the shot that killed Kay cannot have been the shot fired through this velvet scarf. You see that ?
JACKIE. Yes, I see that.
CANON. Two shots we know to have been fired—the one that killed Kay and the one that you fired at Simon Mostyn—but you certainly had not got this scarf wrapped round the pistol.
JACKIE. Of course not.
CANON. Therefore, you see, there must have been a *third* shot . . .
(*There is a pause.*)
JACKIE (*crossing down* C *slowly*). I see what you mean, but . . .
CANON (*following her; interrupting*). Now when we examine the pistol, it appears that two shots have been discharged—but it is quite possible that three shots were actually discharged and one cartridge afterwards replaced to make it look as though only two shots had been fired. If so, when was the third shot fired, and what was the object of it ?
JACKIE (*turning*). I can't even begin to imagine.
CANON. When you were in here last night, was that window open or shut ? (*He indicates the window down* L.)
JACKIE. I don't remember. (*She crosses him and moves up* LC.)
CANON. When I went to bed, it was shut. When I came in here later, it was open. Who opened it ?
JACKIE. What on earth has that got to do with it ?
CANON. A good deal. You see, when I had logically demonstrated to myself that a third shot had been fired, I looked for a third bullet and found it.
JACKIE (*sitting at the table up* L). I still don't see what you mean.
CANON (*moving up* RC). Now consider the French girl, Louise. Before the four of us here last night, Simon, Bessner, Smith, and myself, Louise

went out of her way to make it quite clear that she knew something. She even hinted unmistakably that she had seen the murderer. Why?

JACKIE. Blackmail.

CANON. Blackmail most certainly. But why at that moment? Why a public statement before four people? Why not go to the person concerned privately and say to him or her, "I *know*. How much will you pay for silence?"

JACKIE. I can't imagine. That would certainly have been the sensible way.

CANON. Then why not adopt it? And the answer—the only possible answer—is that for some reason that was impossible. Now do you see how near the truth we are getting?

JACKIE. I suppose I'm stupid, but I don't.

CANON. Louise made her veiled threat in front of four people. That could only mean that the threat was actually made to one of those people.

JACKIE. Oh, I see.

CANON. Louise could have come to me alone, she could have gone to Smith alone, she could have gone to Bessner alone. There was only one person she could not be sure of finding alone—a wounded man with someone constantly in attendance on him—Simon Mostyn.

JACKIE (*rising*). Simon? *Simon?* But you're mad!

CANON. That good-looking, plausible young scoundrel and waster, Simon Mostyn. Simon Mostyn, of whom I had already heard something— so that when I got Kay's letter in Jerusalem telling me she had married him, I hurried here to see for myself and to protect, if I could, the child of my old friend left in my guardianship. I failed to protect her—and that failure lies heavily on me.

JACKIE (*vehemently*). But what you're saying is impossible—absolutely impossible. Simon never left the saloon here after Kay went to bed last night. He was here until I shot him—and after that he couldn't have walked a step. Dr. Bessner says so.

CANON (*nodding his head*). Yes, the sequence seems complete, but it isn't. You fired your pistol, but the bullet went into the floor and not into Simon's knee at all. Simon fell back in his chair and put a handkerchief soaked in some kind of red dye (*he holds up the bottle*) to his knee. And Simon Mostyn had time, while Christina and you and Smith were on the other side of the deck to pick up the pistol from where you had dropped it, run to his wife's cabin, where his wife was lying asleep— drugged, no doubt. Simon shot Kay, ran back here, opened that window, inserted a fresh cartridge, wrapped the pistol in the scarf, that was to avoid scorching, and fired another bullet into his leg. Then he threw scarf, handkerchief, bottle, and pistol in a bundle through that window, and still had time to place his own handkerchief to his knee and was found by Smith and Bessner in exactly the same position as Smith had left him four minutes earlier.

JACKIE (*coming down* LC). It's fantastic!

CANON. It's fantastic—but it's true! (*He comes down* RC *and moves below the table* C.) Simon had one piece of bad luck. Louise didn't drink her invariable camomile tea which had, no doubt, been suitably doctored. Louise was awake. She heard the shot next door. She looked out and saw him. She followed him along here and probably saw him shoot himself. And then, of course, she set out to blackmail him. He reassured her in front of us—and we never saw it. "You'll be all right, Louise. I'll look after you." But in blackmailing him she signed her own death warrant !

JACKIE. Nonsense ! Simon didn't shoot Louise !

CANON. No, he had to rely on the quick wit and understanding of someone else—of his partner. (*With sudden force.*) *You shot Louise, Jacqueline* !

JACKIE. It's a lie !

CANON. He told you here in this saloon that Louise knew the murderer. He told you Bessner had a revolver. You went and got that revolver and shot her.

JACKIE (*crossing to him*). It's a lie !

(CANON PENNEFATHER *seizes her right hand.*)

CANON. Have you ever heard of the moulage test ?

JACKIE (*staring*). Moulage test ?

CANON. If a person has recently discharged a pistol, minute powder grains are embedded in the skin of the hand. They can be extracted with a moulage of wax.

(*With her left hand* JACKIE *grabs the pistol from the table. He catches both her hands. The pistol falls. They stand facing each other. He throws her into the chair* L *of the table. Then he lets her go, stoops and picks up the pistol, putting it in his pocket.*)

JACKIE (*with horror and misery*). Yes—yes—I would have killed you . . . I didn't think it mattered so very much killing Kay—Kay who'd tried to rob me of Simon. And Louise was just a blackmailing harpy. But *you*—you've been kind to me—I like you ! I see now why one must do no murder—it means you aren't safe any more. Once you've learnt how to kill, you'd do it again and again—and again . . . that's true, isn't it ? .

CANON. That is true.

JACKIE. I don't want to kill *you*. You've been kind to me—you've tried to help me . . . that first night—I nearly did what you asked. I nearly got off the boat—gave up the whole thing.

CANON. Would to God you had.

JACKIE. May I tell you how it all happened ?

CANON. Yes, my child, tell me.

JACKIE. It was all true what I told you. Simon was looking for a job. I induced Kay to give him one. Then when she saw him she fell for him. Poor Simon ; he's always wanted money—and he's always been so miserably poor. And here it was being offered to him for the asking. I saw what he felt. I told him he'd better give me up and marry Kay. But he said being the husband of a rich wife was no good to him—and he loved *me*. He said, "If this was a book I'd marry a rich wife and she'd die within the year." And then I saw—I *saw* the idea come into his head ! I taxed him with it. He just laughed and said, "You leave it to me." But I was terrified. Simon's so simple, so terribly optimistic. I knew he'd go about it in some perfectly idiotic way. So I had to help him. You do see that ? I had to help him !

(CANON PENNEFATHER *turns his head away.*)

This plan was mine . . . I thought it was so clever—so absolutely foolproof. He worked it all out. My following them round. Simon's pretence of hating me. It was all worked out down to the last detail—and then you trapped me. I'd never heard of the moulage test.

CANON. Your guilty conscience trapped you. The moulage test would have meant nothing in your case because you had fired that pistol last night. But it will be conclusive in Simon's case because, according to *his* story, he never handled a pistol last night.

JACKIE (*rising*). You mean this is going to hang him ? (*She moves up* C.) Oh, Simon—Simon !

CANON. When the sun shines you cannot see the moon—but the moon is there all the time. Both of you said that to me in almost the same words. I ought to have known then that you were acting together.

JACKIE (*passionately*). I wish Kay was alive. You may not believe it, but it's true. I loved Kay—I know that now. She was so gay and happy—and so generous and warm-hearted ! Oh, if one could only go back.

CANON. You have to go on—not go back.

JACKIE. There's a way out—a quick way and an easy way.

CANON. You mustn't take that way.

JACKIE. You can't stop me.

CANON. To take your own life is as bad as to take that of someone else.

JACKIE. Even if it's already forfeit ?

CANON. Your life is not your own to dispose of. It is only your own to *live*—until the appointed end.

JACKIE. You're cruel.

CANON. No, I am still trying to help you. There are spiritual values of which you know nothing—these next few weeks may be all important to you.

JACKIE (*half mockingly*). To my soul ?

CANON (*seriously*). To your soul.

VOICE (*off; calling*). *Lotus* ahoy. Egyptian police here !

JACKIE (*coming down to the table; up* L *corner*). Won't you give me back my pistol ?

(CANON PENNEFATHER *slowly hands her the pistol.* JACKIE *takes it.*) Aren't you going to stop me ?

CANON. No, the choice must be yours.

JACKIE. I see, the choice must be mine. (*She pauses.*) All right, you win. (*She places the pistol back on the table.*)

(*Voices off grow louder.* CANON PENNEFATHER *takes her hand and they stand together to meet the* EGYPTIAN POLICE OFFICIAL *who enters* R *and salutes.*)

CURTAIN.

FURNITURE AND PROPERTY PLOT.

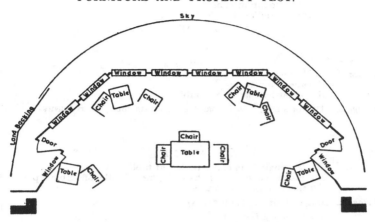

ACT I.

On stage.   Five wicker tables.
Nine wicker chairs.
Magazines, travel folders, and ashtrays on all tables.
Two trays with flywhisks, beads, postcards, scarabs, etc. (*for* BEAD-SELLERS).

Off stage R.   Miss FFOLIOT-FFOULKES' coat ⎫
Small dressing case.   ⎪
Handbag. *In it:* scarab.   ⎬ (CHRISTINA).
Book.   ⎭
Tumbler, half full (SIMON).

Off stage L.   Tray, two tumblers, chit, pencil ⎫
One short drink.   ⎬ (STEWARD).
Two long drinks.   ⎭

Personal.   Miss FFOLIOT-FFOULKES : handbag, spectacles.
KAY : wrap, handbag, mirror, cheque-book.
SIMON : cigarettes, lighter.
CANON : fountain pen.
JACKIE : handbag, pistol.

Note.—All windows shut.

ACT II, SCENE 1.

On stage.   *On table* C : cards dealt for bridge (five in each hand), spare pack, four bridge markers, ashtray.
Miss FFOLIOT-FFOULKES' spectacles (downstage R corner).
Chair set below table C, taken from below table up L. *Over the back of it :* Miss FFOLIOT-FFOULKES' shawl.
On table down L : book, magazines.
On table up L : Knitting, magazines.
Beside chair above table C : portfolio.

Off stage L.   Flit spray.
Tray, two long drinks, one short drink. �⎬ (STEWARD).
One short drink. ⎭

Personal. JACKIE : handbag, pistol.
CANON : fountain pen.
SIMON : handkerchief (red stain).
Note.—All windows shut.

SCENE 2.

On stage. *Strike* pistol.
Open window down L.
Set bullet by chair L of C table.

Off stage L. Doctor's bag. *In it :* bandage, hypodermic (Dr. BESSNER).

ACT III.

On stage. *Replace* chair from below table C at table up L.
Set pistol, velvet scarf, handkerchief, bottle on table up L. Bullet beneath chair L of C table.

Off stage R. Bag of knitting (CHRISTINA).

Off stage L. Doctor's bag (Dr. BESSNER).
Tray with glass of brandy (STEWARD).

Personal. Cigarettes (SIMON).
Note.—All windows open.

LIGHTING PLOT.

ACT I.

No. 1 batten and floats. One circuit 4 medium amber ; one circuit 53 pale salmon.

Back batten, or floods, on sky. One circuit 1 yellow ; one circuit 5 orange ; two circuits 32 blue.

Spots to cover principal acting areas round table C and chairs down R and L, 53 pale salmon ; also to cover tables up R and L, 3 straw.

Lengths outside windows down R and L, amber.

ACT II, SCENES 1 AND 2.

No. 1 batten and floats. One circuit 53 pale salmon ; one circuit 3 straw.
Back batten, or floods, on sky : 32 blue only.
Spots as in ACT I.
Lengths outside windows on check.

ACT III.

Same as ACT I.

(*Note.*—The colours given above are intended only as a guide to the means by which the effect of heat and a brazen sky may be obtained. Those actually employed on the set must be chosen in accordance with the colour scheme of the furnishing and costumes, while those employed to light the sky will be dependent on the particular tone in which the cloth is painted.)

MADE AND PRINTED IN GREAT BRITAIN BY
LATIMER TREND & COMPANY LTD PLYMOUTH
MADE IN ENGLAND